LIFELIKE
PEDAGOGY

ISBN	978-85-910318-1-8
COVER, PUBLISHING AND GRAPHIC DESIGN	MANUELA NEVES
TRANSLATION	ADRIANA CARACCIO MORGAN & NICHOLAS MORGAN
COVER IMAGES	DREAMSTIME

LIFELIKE PEDAGOGY

Marcelo Rodrigues

"To the Sun and a star in the sky"

SUMMARY

PREFACE

This book is the result of several years of reflecting on life and the search for happiness, and some years, although small in numbers but very intense, as an educational director and provider at "Escola do Max."

For those who have never heard of it, "Escola do Max" is an elementary school based in the city of São Paulo, Brazil, in a district called Vila Mariana.

Since its conception, my ideal for this school was to educate happy children. Not through selecting the most cheerful children, but rather because I would use education to make them happier, in the search for physical, emotional and intellectual balance, with freedom being the ever present ingredient.

From its foundation in October 2004 until now, the school has undergone great changes. We have tried several paths in order to attain our goal, and now I can say that we have finally reached it or, at least, I feel that we have reached a new level of education, where the desired happiness seems to reside. This new level made me realize some interesting things. The most obvious among them all is that free and happy children are better learners. Another observation, which was not so obvious, is that this new level aids the development of specific skills, which are very important in the new and ever-changing world in which we live, such as: entrepreneurship, creativity and communication, amongst others.

But the "trick," the main observation that set the foundation for my whole thought process, was that children must not only be educated to be able to deal with life, but rather to use life as an educational tool! And this has even allowed me to call this ideology/methodology, or maybe this movement, as "Lifelike Pedagogy."

We have been attaining excellent results with our students, both regarding learning the school curriculum and their personal development. I was then led to believe that the time has come to share everything I have learnt with other teachers, parents and anybody interested in a higher quality of education.

LIFELIKE ARGUMENTATION

In this book, the reader will find several concepts that are not new and several thinkers have already raised most of the arguments I have included here. Nevertheless, as far as my limited knowledge is concerned, I have not seen the same thoughts, ideas and reflections gathered and applied to the same goal: to offer children a better way to live and learn, learn and live, without having to separate these two things during the teaching-learning process.

But the main reference, from which I collected almost all of my conclusions, was life itself. I invested a lot of time reflecting on life, from the human search for its meaning, until more practical aspects in the daily routine of our lives. A varied, multidisciplinary, and up-to-date bibliography was my starting point. Several unconventional sources were used: reading fashion and life-style magazines, visiting technology websites, observing the movement of executives in the market via business magazines and books, taking part in heated debates over the quality of life and performance at work, reading articles and columns pointing out trends in behavior and the environment, listening to influential people in radio programs, who, in a humorous manner, point out the absurd side of contemporary life, informal conversations with all types of people, amongst others.

Thus, I developed the base for the argument that supports my ideas of what would be an education based on life, or as I like to call it, a "lifelike" education. The argument *per se* is based on the idea I defend, that life must be the reference for everything that is present in education.

I confess that I left the literature specialized in education aside. Not because I have the arrogance to despise it, but because I believe education must walk together with the world, and this has been undergone through such fast changes, and in such surprising directions, that the old concepts are no longer entirely applicable. They are still very important as a technical base, but are no longer a philosophical base for contemporary education. We moved along to the information age, and the Biology age is already being mentioned. The old models must be replaced by something that allows our students to have the ability to keep up with the world in order to reach their personal goals, whatever their desires will be and regardless of the new configuration the world will show them. I am sure of one thing, though: that this configuration will not be the same as today's, let alone that of 20, 30 or 100 years ago.

Therefore, I have to ask the more rigorous readers that may be searching for technical arguments, or meticulously structured arguments, to forgive me, but we now live in an age in which information is available to everyone in real-time, and we deal with it in a completely new manner. Our reality is changeable and truths are temporary and relative. Nowadays, people must be able to conduct an orchestra of information and to form new connections between apparently unrelated things. In one day we must speak English, the following day, it's Chinese. In the modern world, millions of US Dollars are invested based on an idea and nothing else. This may well be old news when this book is finally published, but your mobile phone will connect, via the internet, with your refrigerator in order to see if your favorite yogurt needs to be restocked - but only if your blood sugar levels and your doctor's recommendations allow it. How will the economy and life as a whole be in this new world? Where will our children/students fit in it?

A new way of thinking for a new world. This is what I had in mind when I defended, or at least tried to defend, the philosophy I am presenting in this book, connecting several things to a common core: our life and the search for happiness.

Chapter 1

LIFE AND EDUCATION

During my time in school, I experienced something very interesting, which left an impression on my life. As embarrassing as it may be, I have to confess that I don't remember her name, but she was one of my teachers. To be more specific, she was my English teacher. A certain day, in an informal chat during one of her classes, she very cheerfully presented an important conclusion she learnt from life. Somebody had asked her about the meaning of life and she, intelligently, had studied the question following the reasons for everything she had done. For example: Why do I go to work? So I can make money. And why do I have to make money? So I can buy a house. Why? So I can move out from my small rented apartment. Why? Because I don't like living there. And, thus, she realized that all the paths led to "in order to be happy." So her conclusion was (and she made sure to share it with us): the meaning of life was, pure and simply, to be happy.

I don't know what impressed me the most in that moment. Was it the brilliant conclusion she reached? Was it the simplicity of the analytical process she adopted? Or maybe I was surprised to see her give so much importance to that question, especially taking into consideration the huge contrast between the depth and humanity of her speech in comparison to the coldness and distance of the other teachers I had the pleasure to meet (well, not always).

During my lifetime I have on several occasions made a parallel between my personal decisions and what that English teacher told us on that special day.

But afterwards my thoughts were consumed by a previous question: Does life have a meaning? I needed to find that out (or decide) before trying to give, at least deep down inside me, a meaning for my own life. And I thought a lot and I read a lot about it. I finally (or in principle) concluded that life is a sequence of facts, strongly influenced by, but not decided by, decisions we make. If you decide to live in a dangerous district, you will have a greater chance of having your home invaded or being robbed when taking your car out of the garage. On the other hand, even living in a safe neighborhood, you may be robbed. Our decisions mold our life, but do not define it entirely. There is a random factor, which is entirely out of our control.

My conclusion was that life doesn't come with instructions. Therefore, I felt free to believe that life has no meaning by definition. Life only exists so that we can make whatever we want from it. That is to say that the freedom that any human being has (or should have) to live according to his/her decisions is what provides us with the basis to give the meaning we wish to our lives.

The reader could then ask: "But if we give the meaning we want to our lives, wouldn't we be giving it the meaning that pleases us the most, and therefore what makes us the happiest? Was your teacher right, then?"

Yes and no. Really, what we will look for in the end is happiness, however the path my teacher took to get to this conclusion does not pass through the key aspect of freedom, that defines if we will be able to successfully attribute a meaning to our lives. I will explain it further.

For human beings to be free, it is not enough that they live in a democracy, are financially self-sufficient and are healthy enough to walk around. They need to be free from anguish and fear, their false certainties, their harmful values and prejudices, impositions of friends and family members, their implacable self judgment, the models imposed by society, and from everything else that does not match their personality and most intimate dreams. Then they will be truly free to attribute the meaning they wish for their lives and reach happiness. Otherwise, they will run the risk of having a meaning to their life that does not correspond to their true, honest self, and will be subject to pursue during their life a dream that is not theirs, and therefore, they may drift away from happiness. A person like this will be constantly in doubt and will never be satisfied, always having the sensation that something is missing. But what is really missing is themselves.

Life is full of traps that prevent us from finding ourselves and freeing ourselves. We live in a capitalist meritocracy that pushes us constantly to work, in which we are evaluated for our capacity to generate capital. In parallel, or as a consequence of the system, we are getting increasingly further away from our ideals, values and dreams. We are increasingly being pushed further to believe that we will be happy when we buy the car of the year or that new pair of shoes that is exposed in the shop window. The problem is that happiness doesn't come with the new acquisition and we transfer all our expectations to the next purchase, in a financially ascending spiral that means nothing as far as helping the fullness of personal satisfaction.

We are moving increasingly further from ourselves, we are all becoming too similar and we unmercifully judge those who try to be different, maybe due to the risk they represent of us realizing that we do not know who we are. This can be scary!

If we do not know ourselves, how could we attribute meaning to our lives? What is the criterion to be used? As painful as the process may be for some of us (and I include myself in this group), we have to feel all our emotions if we want to be happy, as the car of the year will not come with a bottle of happiness in the glove compartment.

People's true value

But what does all this has to do with education?

The most concerned readers will answer this question with the reflection that they certainly had while reading the ideas above: "What can I do to prevent my students from falling into this social trap and be fully free in their thoughts and feelings?"

We need to rethink the school as a whole. The contemporary school is not only a participant in this degenerative process, but it collaborates a lot with it, forming citizens who are increasingly more focused on their financial performance and getting increasingly more distant from themselves.

Some capitalist meritocrats could mention the social losses generated by a freer society, in constant contact with its emotions, pursuing its dreams, totally detached from performance evaluation. My answer to them may be summarized in only one word: "inspiration." Let's imagine a society formed by people who trust their ideals, are inspired by their emotions and free from the exacerbated consumerism or from the frenetic and disloyal competition. If freed from prejudice, envy, fear, arrogance, pre-formatted models, amongst other evils, what would people be capable of?

My view is that, in fact, we would not have social losses, but a huge gain which would change the order of things. And I also state that if this achievement belonged to only one individual, involved in our current model of life, even so his achievements would be gigantic and, as a consequence, also his gains, not only for society, but mainly for himself, as he would certainly be a lot closer to happiness than we ever dreamt possible.

The current school does not favor the emergence of characters such as Martin Luther King, Baron of Mauá, John Lennon, Marie Curie, Albert Einstein, Shakespeare, Ayrton Senna, Thomas Edison, amongst so many others. Let's imagine how many others would have stood out in the same manner, or even more, if they had attended a school that listened to them, allowed them to express their imaginative minds, that gave space to grow, that provoked them, stimulated them, that gave them the self confidence and all the tools necessary to reach their dreams, even if this dream were only a football game in school. A school which gave these people the freedom to feel and know themselves, so that they could free themselves from models and judgments, being able to follow and live their wonderful dreams.

My dear reader, what could all these people have been able to do for themselves and for the world?

A TASTE FOR THE UNKNOWN

The more we evolve in our "lifelike" proposal, the more I see that all the answers are in the student. Many times, teachers struggle to find out how to make their students learn the contents required by the Ministry of Education, but the answer is right in front of their eyes: in the student. The teachers need to become more involved with themselves and with their students. Only a common experience may open the doors for full and efficient communication.

Teachers must understand, before anything else, that they do not teach, they learn with their students. Teachers and the school as a whole should not be a source of knowledge, but a source of inspiration. The school must help the student to look for the tools in order to build whatever he/she desires, without being afraid of the unknown. After all this is what life is all about: discovering, exploring, understanding, feeling, experiencing. The highly desired happiness passes through freedom, and the school needs to free itself from its fears, prejudices and arrogance. And, as soon as possible, from a pedagogical plan that is old, set in stone, out of context and discon-nected from the life we live today and, especially, the life our students will live tomorrow.

Nobody can be prepared for life by being excluded from it, simply pretending that there is not a whole and incredible world out there, in constant movement and with endless opportunities to learn and explore. Even with their knowledge being based on scientific achievements, schools have forgotten the reason why human be-ings learn, why science and men evolve. Human curiosity, with the desire to understand the universe, to dominate the environment, the need to survive thanks to our capacity, is the engine that moves us towards knowledge. Schools must follow this same mechanism. The student must learn in order to live and learn how to live. Life must enter school through all its doors and windows, inspiring students and teachers to exceed themselves, not in order to receive merits, but to reach their dreams, whatever they may be.

Schools nowadays are boring! They discourage everyone, be they students, teachers or principals. They manage to discourage even the parents, who do not feel encouraged to take part in their children's activities, contributing with the very important affective aspect, which would help students grow as students and people.

The current learning model used in schools is inefficient and fake. Most students do not remember what the test they had the day before was about, even after receiving a satisfactory grade. The subject is not interesting to them and they only feel pressure from society as a whole to get the expected grades and evaluations. What could be expected from a professional that studied out of obligation? What evolution may be expected from a person who believes that learning is boring and difficult?

That is the reason why we see so many adults, in unfortunately increasing numbers, interested only in celebrity magazines and futile subjects. Or, on the other hand, they are fully, and blindly, focused on the unstoppable search for more and more money, as an attempt to attribute meaning to their empty lives, forgetting themselves, their families, their friends, always complaining about their lack of time and quality of life, without making any effort to change their life style.

Let's be better than that! Let's teach our students that there is a whole world out there, and we can do that by bringing this world to the classroom and, at the same time, taking the classroom to the world out there. Let's bring the world to our lives.

THE TEACHER'S ROLE

In practical terms, what I understand as connecting school to the world is to teach students via actually experiencing real problems and enterprises. We are talking about giving freedom to the students to create, and let them discover what they should learn in order to reach their goals. Further on, I will present a methodology that allows all these concepts to be applied in a practical and efficient manner.

THE EXPECTANT-TEACHER

The role of the teacher must change radically. Instead of dispensing knowledge, hoping that students absorb something, teachers must, before anything else, have fun. Yes, fun. They need to enjoy and love what they do. In my experience, what motivates anyone to become a teacher is the affectionate involvement that emerges from the relationship with other human beings and the pride taken in their personal evolution and achievements. But how is it possible to reach these two sources of satisfaction if the students are passive in the whole process? How is it possible to develop an affectionate connection in a relationship based only on authority? How can one be proud of achievements when the student doesn't even show the desire to struggle? Or could we consider a high grade on a test as a personal achievement? Personally, I believe this is too little. Down with mediocrity!

We are talking of student and teacher, united, based on pedagogical freedom guaranteed by school and parents, which allows them to imagine real enterprises and struggle together to reach them, searching for the necessary knowledge to overcome each obstacle, dealing with psychological aspects such as frustration, overcoming fears, socialization, amongst others, at each step improving their skills of creativity, leadership, communication, logical-mathematical thinking and emotional intelligence.

In such a process, teachers will most certainly become motivated and will transfer their motivation on to the student. Consequently, the students will be a lot more interested, encouraging the teachers to really put their hear in the process.

The teachers will no longer be central figures, becoming expectant instead, admiring the initiative, achievement, each step their students take towards their goals.

THE STIMULATING TEACHER

Like a coach, who yells at the team the whole time, stimulating them to give their best and to believe in victory, teachers should show their students that they believe in them, that they support them, that they will assume the risks with them in order to reach their goals and dreams.

THE GUIDING TEACHER

As a wise person, the teacher must offer advice, showing the possible threats and opportunities that may be found along the way, but the teacher must never make a decision on the students' behalf. No one can learn in life following scripts. Taking risks is something necessary and teachers must guide their students during their journey, helping them face obstacles, so that they can get to know themselves and face the situations with courage and strength.

THE PROVOCATIVE TEACHER

Many feelings may come from a teacher's provocation. The teacher must prod their students so that they move, think, ask, question, and argue: all valid actions in the discovery of life and the world.

THE CHALLENGING TEACHER

This doesn't mean challenging in the sense of stirring up op-position towards their students. Teachers should suggest challenges to be met together with the students. The teacher should show that they can do more, can go beyond what they think they can and that their teacher believes in them to the point of suggesting that they advance.

THE COLLABORATIVE TEACHER

A partner. This term can describe the teacher who collaborates, who does their share, who works together with their students, hands on. Not in the sense of replacing the students, but doing with the students, being part of the group.

THE FACILITATING TEACHER

Students are not always ready for a challenge that arises. The teacher must be the regulator of the challenge, so that it doesn't become a factor to discourage the students, being too easy or too difficult. In certain situations, as it would defeat the purpose if the students didn't manage to advance, the teacher may facilitate some passages.

THE STUDENT'S ROLE

For the student educated in a "lifelike" proposal, their role is to dream and suggest challenges, persevere looking for a goal that they intend to reach. They will have to learn how to work in groups, respecting the opinion and desires of their work colleagues. Democracy and companionship becoming ways to make decisions and a collaborative attitude is essential.

The frustration, as part of life, must be tolerated and overcome, in order to accept defeats and to fight for the next victories that may arise. The student must become more mature to deal with unforeseen challenges.

Students educated in a learning philosophy based on the experience must wake up to life, realizing that when they desire something, it is within their reach, provided they make an effort to achieve it. They must believe in themselves to overcome several obstacles presented by their enterprises. They will not be scared of talking to people, either via the telephone or in person, after all they will need to do it several times in order to obtain quotes, authorizations, collaborations, etc.

These people will see themselves and the world with great enthusiasm, as something accessible. Regardless of which route is chosen, they will know that nothing is unobtainable, as they will be accustomed to looking for resources and obtaining information.

They will be people who believe in other people, after all, they will work in teams, helping and receiving collaboration from all kinds of people, and this will open them up to companionship and friendship. But they will not be fools, as experience will show them that it is not possible to blindly believe everything they see or hear, as there are people with good and bad intentions.

THE EXPERIENCE AS A PATH FOR PERSONAL EVOLUTION

In my proposal called "lifelike," I highlight how important it is to praise life and our relationship with it, looking for happiness.

The contents required by The Ministry of Education are necessary and so they should be required. In fact, I believe the requirements aren't enough in comparison to the opportunity offered to any school. In the "lifelike" approach, the mandatory contents should be naturally developed within the challenges raised by the students. After all, it is the necessary basic knowledge to build the whole contemporary society and the students will inevitably deal with it.

However, much more than covering the mandatory content, the "lifelike" approach aims to form people that believe in themselves, in life and in the world. They feel like they own the world and are capable of overcoming any challenge that may come their way in the pursuit of their dreams.

The school must be connected with the planet so that the students may learn for life, and through life.

A VERY SPECIAL HUMAN BEING

In this chapter, I may be taking more risks. I apologize to all psychologists, psychiatrists, psychopedagogists and other professionals who are noble enough to try and understand the labyrinth of the human mind. I apologize for the great simplification that I will make of important emotional processes which occur in our minds, which I'm aware that are infinitely more complex than what I will write here. I ask you to understand the story of my life, everything I have noticed in the relationship between teacher and student, lives of friends and colleagues that I have seen being wasted, the incredible ideas lost due to lack of support, the monumental effort made by many people to overcome their total lack of faith in themselves, among other such nonsense. All these things show me that we have no time for deep analyses or arguments. I believe that the subject I will deal with in this chapter, for many in an irresponsible manner, will be, for others, the starting point to, in a more pragmatic manner, offer their students the minimum psychological balance necessary so that they may at least try something they dream about.

There is no time to waste! We need to act now, firmly and swiftly. Today's school, its teachers, principals, parents and other involved parties need to understand, even if superficially, what makes a successful human being. With that, their learning may be channeled inside their students' hearts and minds!

Apologies done, as is the important warning, we must move along.

A SUCCESSFUL HUMAN BEING

In the lectures and training sessions I give my team at "Escola do Max," I like to present an imaginary young person (man or woman, I'll just use the masculine pronoun for the sake of simplification) that would have been educated in a "lifelike" proposal or, even better, what I desire for my students and children.

"We have a young man, in his early twenties, happy, intelligent, dynamic, creative, idealist, a responsible citizen, capable of being in any situation and talking to anyone. He has dreams and is struggling to achieve them. He is not afraid, is open-minded and involved with the world. A very "cool" guy, focused on his objectives."

What would be the capacity of a young person like that? What type of achievements may that man reach in his life? What would it be like to live in a society formed by people like this?

The reader must pay special attention to the fact that a person with the above profile is not pre-formatted. It's not about creating a mold and having all children and teenagers coming out the same. In education, I defend the process of polishing, not fabrication. It is very important to realize that the characteristics listed above are, in fact, immensely useful skills in order to have that person express himself as he wishes, showing his own personality, deciding which direction he should take in his career, where he should live, what he should eat, with whom he should have relationships, and so forth. The skills described above are a set of attributes that guarantee that that young man will be able to climb any mountain, regardless of size, location or level of difficulty. A human being with the skills listed above can achieve anything they wish for, go in any direction and overcoming any obstacle.

It is important to say that the description for a young person educated within a "lifelike" philosophy doesn't include attributes such as: "sound knowledge in trigonometry," "full command of the reproduction process of the anellides" or, who knows, a "critical view of the Swedish industrialization process." The students in this approach "experience" learning, they learn things and develop abilities which are pertinent to the world they live in, not only in the local scale, but globally. Certainly, this young person would not be able to describe the Swedish industrialization process, but he will have great pleasure in discussing his views on the opportunities and threats that come out of a significant drop in the interest rates in the United States or in China. Unless he chooses a profession in the areas of Mathematics or Science, such as Engineering, trigonometry won't be his strong suit. However, it will be very easy for him to carefully analyze the different loans offered by his bank to buy the necessary equipment to start his own business, even evaluating the impacts each plan would have on his new enterprise's business plan. If he didn't choose to work in the public health or environmental control area, probably he won't have a deep knowledge on the reproductive process of the anellides, but, without any doubt, he will definitely know how much global warming may affect the climate of his country and the probable impacts on agriculture, or how to manage emergencies in large cities.

In a nutshell, this young man would be a person in control over the world around him, knowing everything he needs to know in order to extract everything life can give him. But, at the same time, he would be prepared to advance in more specific studies if necessary, if, for example, he is hired to manage the environmental impact of a major industrial plant that belongs to a Swedish multinational company, where knowledge about the Swedish industrialization process, the reproduction of the anellides and, in some way that I wasn't able to imagine, advanced trigonometry might be useful for him.

The important thing is to learn how to feel, learn how to question, learn how to learn, learn how to make things happen, learn how to live! In the "lifelike" proposal, this is the goal. In an approach focused on polishing human beings so that they are apt to achieve their dreams, life is content, classroom and teacher, all at the same time.

Some could ask (especially the most conservative and concerned parents): "What about the college entrance exam?"

Firstly, it's important to mention that the college entrance exam ("vestibular", in Brazilian Portuguese), as carried out nowadays, is condemned, and there are several studies currently being taken regarding possible alternatives to it. However, we must be cautious and prepare our students for the possibility that things may remain as they currently are. Even so, I'm very confident to say that for students educated under the "lifelike" proposal, this exam is the least important thing. Despite its difficulty and impact on the life of youngsters, the "lifelike" students aren't afraid of the "vestibular." We're talking about youngsters that are accustomed to face daily and real challenges, overcoming their own fears and social pressures, understanding the world that surrounds them and, especially, believing in themselves. For them, the "vestibular" is only a test (in fact). These students will be more apt to associate knowledge to facts and actual problems, they'll be more sagacious to perceive "trick questions," will put their memory to better use, associating facts to times, specific information to broader contexts, will write more fluently, and these are all skills that make a lot of difference in the "vestibular," especially in the essay exam. But, above all, they'll be more confident in themselves in order to be calmer, being more attentive and achieving better results.

Despite agreeing that the issue is relevant, I must confess that analyzing the "lifelike" proposal with the "vestibular" in mind is to ignore the giant personal gains from the students, which is impossible to evaluate in simple written exams.

Thus, in order to clarify the question a little further, I'd like to detail the vision of this young person that I mentioned before, discussing each section presented in the description.

SKILLS OF A WINNER

"A young man, in his early twenties..."

At this age, this young man has finished University, that is to say he's starting to work and entering his full adult life. At this time, he's ready to show what his purpose in life is and what he'll do with everything he has learnt so far. It's time to put his life plan into action.

"...happy..."

How can one state that this young man is happy?

Not considering isolated problems, regarding family, health conditions, romantic relationships, etc, I can say he's happy as he has, up until now, enjoyed his freedom. This young man was educated to realize that life and the world belong to him, and he has to take a look within himself in order to decide upon his next steps. Therefore, he has faced adverse situations, enemies, threats and his own demons, because, if he had been exposed to life, he has also been exposed to himself. And, dear reader, I may say that, although via merely personal and emotional bases, when you are near yourself, and when you deeply know yourself, when you don't run from your own emotions, happiness is inevitably within our reach.

Also, happiness is not a gift, something carried in our DNA. To be happy is an act of observation, reflection and respect. A state reached by thinking and taking the right decisions, using one's own references. Happiness is built by each one of us, every step we take towards ourselves, assessing the risks, the opportunities, our strengths and weaknesses.

Students prepared to live do all this with self-confidence and joy. They are the personification of the difference between learning how to do things and doing by instinct.

"...intelligent..."

IQ tests don't assess a person's intellectual capacity not even superficially. Based on important papers from specialists in human intelligence, we can see that the human being presents, in fact, multiple forms of intelligence. Among them, language, logical-mathematical thinking, emotional intelligence, etc. Although the classification proposed until today still needs to be improved, we may see that other forms of thinking also have a strong influence on our decisions and search for answers, besides only those involved with logic, mathematics and spatial perception, which are commonly assessed in the IQ tests.

Thus, what is necessary for a "brain performance" is to look for the best possible balance between the different forms of intelligence, making the most of those in which one is good and learn to apply one's own intelligence standard in real situations, especially when one is dealing with tight deadlines, scarce resources, lack of information and support, etc. - which means most of the situations we have to face everyday. Or do we overcome our daily obstacles searching for the next geometrical figure in a sequence supplied in a questionnaire? Life is infinitely more complex than that! And having a set of "*intelligences*" makes all the difference.

Therefore, children educated for life and through life are more intelligent than the average, in the broadest possible meaning that the term "intelligence" may have.

"...dynamic..."

While looking for the meaning of the term "dynamic" in the Merriam-Webster Dictionary, I found some interesting things. Among them: energetic, forceful.

Although the words above speak for themselves, it's interesting to highlight the meanings we found within the context we're analyzing.

In the world and in life, nothing lasts forever. Even the universe is in a continuous movement and change, in a cycle, also finite, of birth, development and death. After all, we know that the universe had a beginning and is moving towards an end. Such as everything else, we're involved in a completely dynamic environment. What was truth yesterday is no longer valid today, and so we're forced (or blessed) to follow life and the changing world.

And, regarding the sociocultural and socioeconomic context, changes seem to have become accelerated. Nowadays, mainly due to technology, we live in a frenetic world that bombards us with an almost infinite amount of information and transformation. Everybody needs to deal with everything in a natural and agile manner, absorbing the changes at great speed, and this must be done both in their professional and personal capacity.

The students who become accustomed to the actual rhythm of life, instead of the teacher's or the school's rhythm, internalize a process of constant personal evolution that will not only benefit them in the competitive job market, but in the search and maintenance of happiness.

"...idealist..."

A person without an ideal is a poor person. Whatever the ideal is. Whatever the goal of a person's life is, it's important that a sense is given to the fact of being alive.

Students who are properly inserted in reality, who perceive the world around them, who believe in their skills, who love life and are happy, will never put aside everything they built within themselves in order to "go with the flow." They want to conduct the orchestra or at least be part of it. They want to leave their contribution, their mark.

The "lifelike" students don't defend the school's values, don't adopt the teachers' values, don't accept being manipulated by their families. They believe in their own opinions, which are a result of long reflections and observation and, based on them, they will change the world if they decide to do so.

"...a responsible citizen..."

Why would he want to harm his environment and society? The place where he'll raise his children and play with his grandchildren.

Having been educated to work both individually and in groups – after all, certain goals are impossible to be reached alone – the students realize how important the collective group is, as well as the responsible contribution from each individual. They understand why rules exist and their key importance to the order. Besides, the students who perceive the natural processes be they biological, physical, chemical, social or economic, but in a real and "lifelike" manner, beyond the book or notebook, will develop a long-term view. These students realize that their future achievements will be a consequence of them making the right decisions in the present.

In education, regarding ethics and citizenship, we must go a lot further than what we've been doing today. We need to internalize in children the reasons why these aspects are so important. The students need to realize the relevance of the impact that their attitudes will have on themselves. After all, the attitude of each one of us reflects in our environment and, consequently, affects us. More than learning how to be a good citizen, the students must "feel" what being a citizen is like, in their own skin.

"...capable of being in any situation and talking to anyone..."

In order to have free access to the world, one needs self-esteem, before anything else. One can't be intimidated by adverse situations and flinch in the face of challenges. Self-esteem shows us that we're all the same, that there are no inferior people in the world, but inferior views and attitudes. Thus, one has to know and value oneself, before taking part in any environment or joining anyone's company.

However, some things ease the process and open opportunities to live with several types of people. The "experience," or as many call it, the "baggage" of life, that huge set of information we collect and carry throughout our life, allows us to have better judgment on how to behave, what to say and when, how we should dress for each occasion, etc.

With a minimum and varied cultural knowledge, we'll be able to start talking to people, expressing our thoughts and participating, sharing opinions and criticizing facts or comments.

We could also add etiquette, table manners, niceties and minor rules to community living in several types of environments and cultures.

We all know how many doors open for those who are well related, that know how to transmit the proper and desired image wherever they go. We also know the advantages of communicating and selling one's own set of skills. Thus, we must breathe life into the school, so that students learn with it and acquire at least part of this "baggage" of life or "experience" that may open so many doors for them.

"...He has dreams and is struggling to achieve them..."

To be honest with you, it was very difficult for me to write about this part of the description. The reason for this was my view on the theme "dreams." For me, people in general think small. Thus, I even managed to write some paragraphs full of powerful phrases and a lot of arguments to support my opinion. However, I realized I wasn't being clear, taking the reader to a simple and very fair question: "Who do you think you are to judge if a person's dream is small or big?".

That was when I deleted everything I had written and realized I should follow another path in order to present my point of view. So I started to look on the internet for some reference or inspiration that could help me clarify my thoughts. I started my research by listing what usually people dream of. I found many interesting things on several websites where people have no fear of expressing their thoughts. Initially I wasn't interested in getting scientific information or technical references regarding the theme. I was only trying to listen "what people are saying," and I found some interesting things, such as:

"Go to Paris"
"Meet the members of Kiss"
"Make a living from my profession"
"Go to Venice"
"Dance flamenco"
"Write a book"
"Take singing lessons"
"Travel the world"
"Go to London"
"Become a veterinarian"
"Build a shelter for street kids"
"Go to Egypt"
"Get an apprenticeship in Archeology"
"Become an actress"
"Be a mother"
"Have money"
"Go to University"

There were also more generic dreams related to:

"Peace" (personal, local or global)
"Money" (financial independence, wealth, etc.)
"Health"
"Love"
"Happiness"
"Time" (quality of life, longevity, eternity, etc.)

Before I present my point of view, I'd like to ask the reader to read again the dreams above and think:

How many people end their lives without having their dreams come true, such as go to Paris or write a book?

Are those dreams big or small?

Honestly, I can't accept the fact that a person can consider a trip to Paris as something unattainable, or, at least, difficult enough to put it in the category of "dreams of a lifetime." What could we say about writing a book, then?!

Dear reader, I live in a country where a steelworker in the Greater São Paulo area became the President of the Republic and was reelected! (I apologize for the amount of exclamations, but for me they're extremely necessary).

We'll avoid here any political debate; this is not about an admiration for the Workers' Party in Brazil or their cause. It's about looking at a human being, from humble origins, with little education, but full of will and self-esteem to put him at the highest position in the country. Nothing held this man back, not even the consecutive defeats he faced in several elections.

Someone might say: "But to write a book, one needs not only the will, but also education, knowledge, financial resources, amongst other things." I'd fully agree if we're talking about getting ready and writing a book in only one week, but we're talking here about a person's dream. That thing that he wishes more than anything else during his whole life.

I have no fear in affirming that, even if this is a dream of a lifetime of an illiterate in the Northeastern backlands, it isn't impossible and, with dedication, it could become reality in little over a decade.

The problem is that people don't believe in themselves, they don't think they can achieve their dreams. As they don't believe they can, they put what should be a "wish" in the "dream" category, and send it to the infinite, with little hope of reaching it one day. And for doing that, they don't fight to achieve it, as they don't feel capable. This generates frustration and then conformism.

In order to share my view of how things could be different, I'd like to present the following story:

THE ILLITERATE WRITER

João Guerreiro[1] is a poor illiterate man from the Northeastern backlands. With a strong personality, João Guerreiro is a privileged man.

Guerreiro, 31 years old now, was born with the incredible capacity to never allow his self-esteem to be shaken in any situation: not the extreme poverty in the Northeastern backlands in a prolonged drought, not the daily social humiliation, hunger, violence or any other source of disgrace in his life. Nothing that happens to João Guerreiro has the power to shake the faith he has in himself. A dreamer (and a fighter), he decided he'll be a writer and will write a book that will be read by lots of people. João already knows what the subject will be: he will talk about the hunger that everybody faces in that region forgotten by the government and society.

When he told his family and friends about his decision, João Guerreiro sat down in order to relax and have more concentration. He wanted to memorize every detail of that scene. His friends and relatives laughed really hard, making fun of that illiterate poor man that wants to be a writer. His nephew Pedrinho, 3 years old, impersonated him perfectly: "I'll be a *witer*," which made his absurd statement even funnier. João Guerreiro decided to memorize the scene perfectly in order to invert the roles, and laugh with the same intensity when the day comes when he'll enter through that door with a box of copies of his book.

A lunatic, a dreamer or somebody that makes things happen? The fact is that João Guerreiro said goodbye to everyone, and, with a rucksack on his back, hitchhiked to the capital, despite being really hungry.

Two years later, he sent a letter to his family – written by a friend, truth be told – telling that he had been promoted to foreman in the same company where he found a job when he arrived in the capital. He worked only to get food and a place to sleep, but he showed

---

1 Guerreiro is a surname in Brazil, which translates to "warrior," "fighter".

so much dedication that the contractor, for pity or recognition, gave him the opportunity to be a foreman, after all Guerreiro, as they called him, was a real fighter. He was a very fast learner and never got tired. Everybody liked him at work, especially for that crazy idea of becoming a writer and creating stories at lunch time.

Some day, Guerreiro was called to work in Rio de Janeiro. The contractor for whom he worked had been invited to put a team together and build some sheds. João Guerreiro got his things together and went with him. It would be a great opportunity to write, or to dictate a new letter for the family and friends, telling them the news.

João Guerreiro hadn't even have the time to see the natural beauty of the city when he was given part of his dream. One of the workers lived in the city and told him he was attending a literacy program for adults in a public school in the district he lived. His colleague needed to repeat a little more times than he wanted to, in a very detailed manner, how to get to the NGO, which was the entity that registered those interested. Guerreiro wasn't going to miss that opportunity, after all, that program was teaching people like him to read and write and, most importantly, for free! And that's how João Guerreiro became "João das Letras"[1], who was almost fired several times for spending too much time with his writing and too little with the masonry, his specialty. At that time, "João das Letras" himself wrote his first letter for his family. He was cheeky enough to say that all that was missing now was to write the book.

Two more years and "João das Letras[2]" had already read everything he could, from novels to work codes. João had really learnt a lot of things. However, the most important thing he had learnt was that, in order to publish a book, one needs to be liked by an editor. And so João spent the next three years of his life between his married life, the daughter that had been born, his work on the building site and the post, as he posted daily a curriculum and a handwritten letter containing details about his great efforts and responsibility at work. The letters contained his sad story, that's true, but João was

---

2 "Letras" means "letters".

determined to find a job in a publishing house, even if it was cleaning the lavatories.

On a certain day, João received a call on his mobile phone, that he had purchased with the money he was paid at the building sites. It was somebody from a mid-sized publishing house, offering a job as a gardener, only part time. The person said that one of the managers was moved when he received the 9th letter that João had sent them, as he understood his dream because he had gone through something similar and also came from the backlands. Though concerned with the salary, a lot smaller than what he was able to get on the building sites, "João das Letras" accepted the invitation and celebrated with his wife and daughter the fact that he had managed to work in a publishing house. The dream of his book was a lot closer now, and he sent another letter to his friends and relatives, now typed on the computer by his neighbor's son, who worked in an internet café.

It was no surprise when "João das Letras," or simply "Das Letras" as people used to call him now, was promoted to maintenance manager in the publishing house's new building. Three years after he had started as a gardener, João, besides being an excellent employee, was a great friend to everybody, especially the office people, where he did a top-notch job, after all he wanted to have a good relationship with the publishers.

But it was when he was blessed with the opportunity of making a hydraulic service in the house of Carlos Cunha, the editor in chief, that João's dream started to come true. While he explained the best way to do the work, including excellent tips regarding the maintenance of the swimming pool, João took the opportunity to comment on his dream and the day when his family made fun of him.

"But you were an illiterate when you were 31?"

This was the cue for João to summarize his life, narrating in clear language and poetic intonation the most important parts. João, at that time, put his lips, tongue, vocal chords, brain, heart and soul to work together, like a symphony to touch the heart of the company's editor in chief and, who knows, get the opportunity of a lifetime. And that was what he got:

"Das Letras, we need to publish your story."

Time went by and Guerreiro forgave, deciding not to make fun of friends and relatives, but he was proud and emotional when he entered his family's old home, with the box of copies of his book that, although it was no best seller, had enough profit for the publishing house to decide to print the second edition after some time.

He helped several friends and relatives improve their life with the money he received from other books he wrote, those directed to the self-help segment, where he tried to teach people to believe in their dreams, regardless of the difficulties they may come across. He loved to read the letters sent by the readers, contaminated with João Guerreiro's strength, or "Das Letras".

The above story was created to represent my view of how things are possible and dreams can be reached. In the narrative, I was very careful to exclude the "luck" factor during João Guerreiro's achievements. Each step he achieves is fruit of several things – especially determination, effort and courage, but little luck. Or is it possible to think that opportunities that came up couldn't come up at another time and context? Our life is surrounded with opportunities and we would be a lot more successful, in any sense, if we noticed them more often. How many opportunities come and go without us even noticing them?

João Guerreiro was successful because he was a fighter.

"All of us are as big as our dreams"
Fernando Pessoa

"If you can dream it, you can do it"
Walt Disney

"We are what we think. All that we are arises with our thoughts.
With our thoughts, we make the world"
Buddha

I truly believe that any human being can achieve practically anything. This is our essence, what makes us special, what really gives meaning to our existence.

So, let's go back to our young man that has dreams and is struggling to reach them. If he really knows the paths of life, believes in himself and works hard, he'll be able to achieve his dreams.

A "lifelike" education, that deals with the students' psychological aspects so that he believes in himself and that gives him really useful tools for the world in which he lives and will live, will make several "Guerreiros".

What could João Guerreiro have reached if he had been properly loved, fed and educated?

"...He is not afraid, is open-minded and involved with the world..."

In a certain way, to be open to the world, not being afraid of it, is connected to the analysis that we have previously discussed, about believing in himself. High self-esteem frees the person to face challenges, favoring a more open attitude towards life and the world. The reader will see how important self-esteem is for me, and how much this must be felt and worked on by the teacher during the activities with the students.

We fear what we don't know. The students educated in the "lifelike" approach know the world, know how things work and do not feel intimidated. As they have experienced several situations under the supervision of the teachers and the "lifelike" school, the students have perceived risky situations and behavior, learning how to avoid them.

Also, it's very important to highlight the fact that the students are "connected to the world." This means to be attentive to what happens around them, recognizing trends, styles, changes and anything that may represent an opportunity or threat in their lives. The "lifelike" students understand that the world is very dynamic and that they must be connected to it full time.

But how do the "lifelike" students manage to stay connected to the world?

In any way possible. I'll list some:

CONTACT WITH PEOPLE

The students must learn about several cultures and societies, must understand a little about human psychology, adopting the right attitude for every type of people they interact with, using the right approach, the most appropriate language, besides developing good sensitivity to understand people's reactions, which will make it a lot easier to relate to people.

It's not enough to only speak with people their own age, they need to feel comfortable to enjoy the contact with their friends' parents, the neighbors of their friends' parents, the man at the newsstand, their teachers, the secretary at school, with the man in the bakery, the bank teller, the manager, the waiter, their friends on networking sites within and outside their own country. In summary, as many people as possible. You never know where the next creative idea will come from, the next relevant information, the next friendship, the next loving relationship. Everybody needs to be open to the world, and people are by far the best way to do this.

We must encourage our students to have contact with people from different religions, races, age groups, social classes, opinions, etc.

SPEAK ENGLISH

Nowadays we already know how important it is to speak English, not due to any Americanism or importing of a foreign culture, but just to be part of this planet! Anywhere you go, maybe except for France, people speak English.

Not taking into consideration any geopolitical issue, the world is becoming smaller, cultural frontiers are almost nonexistent and major companies are global.

I don't think we need to waste paper here talking about the internet.

Therefore, the "lifelike" students, In order to be able to fully explore the world, must speak English. Thus, I include here that a "lifelike" school must also be bilingual.

HAVE COMMAND OF THE WRITTEN LANGUAGE

Be it Portuguese, English or any other language, students must have outstanding writing and reading skills.

In reading, the students must have the skills to read between the lines, to understand the author's thoughts, capture his feelings, his opinions. They should be able to perceive details that not even the author had realized he had given. They should also associate the profile of the author to what is being read, perceiving possible interests and limitations in the author's arguments. Therefore, with an attentive and critical posture, they will not let themselves be taken by the rhetoric and will separate facts from opinions, adopting only those things that interest them.

In writing, they should be able to do the other way round, articulate their ideas very well, using the words in a coherent, intelligent and affectionate manner. They must explore their emotions and those of their readers, leading them as an admirable leader.

NEW TECHNOLOGY

Younger people are naturally open to new technology. We believe the biggest challenge here is the school and the teachers also being open to it, so they can bring all the most modern tools to the classroom or to the backpacks of their students during their explorations throughout life.

The school needs to become up-to-date, in order to incorporate new technology in their pedagogical goals, so that they can teach students the best way to explore it, encouraging their creativity to search for new forms to use it to their benefit.

There is no reason to fear Messenger, Skype, Orkut, Second Life or any other new technology which will come up before this book is published. Some teachers fear e-mail!!!

In order to prepare students connected to the world, teachers and the school must also be connected to it. They should have the courage to explore new technology and assume risks in the incredible changes of paradigms that it brings to the teaching process and to daily life in general.

But teachers should be very careful! This is not about teaching the students, but learning with them. Exploring technology with your students and reflecting with them: "If this technology does this, how can we use it positively?".

PRESS

The students who separate the political interests in everything they read, listen or watch, who understand what is fact and what is opinion, what is a trend and what is fad, will be using the press wisely.

The large journalistic groups in the world are still the best source from which to get up to date with what is occurring in the world, but one needs to be careful in order not to become just another face in the crowd. The press directs the mass and the students must understand these mechanisms and make their own judgment and opinion.

To compare different views about the same fact may make things clearer, and connected students will always do that in order to find the truth in things.

This will not be an easy task, especially because the teachers should also review their own attitude towards the press before helping their students interpret facts, more than texts.

LOOK AT THEMSELVES

Trust in themselves to the point of allowing themselves to change their opinion is key. To be the owner of the truth, to be blinded by arrogance, is the quickest way to fail.

To be open and connected to the world is allowing oneself to acquire new visions that help building a real image of things. The students should learn to combine different points of view in order to better develop their view of things.

Prejudice must never be allowed, in order to respect all opinions, after all it's impossible to know where the comment that will help to find the answer to one's problem will come from.

These are some of the ways to remain open to the world, which must be combined so that the students may learn to interact with life and the planet, in order to extract everything one needs to achieve their dreams, regardless of what they are.

"...A very "cool" guy, focused on his objectives."

In order to finish our description of the "lifelike" young man, who is ready to live his adult life to its fullest, I would like to talk a little about how he positions himself before the world.

I used the slang "cool" here in order to describe a person that doesn't follow pre-established patterns or that, at least, doesn't unknowingly follow them. The "lifelike" young man is cool because he has his own conception of beauty, style, opinion and behavior. It's not a hippie-like posture, which would also be preformatted by someone, but that's about following his own patterns and style.

The teachers must be careful not to judge the students according to their own preferences, but rather stimulate the students to find their own. The student should not follow opinions from the teachers, school or family, but their own opinions.

They know what they like and what they want, and they know what in their behavior may be positive or not to achieve their goals.

Also, somebody who is focused on their goals isn't a selfish person. After all, the "lifelike" students understand how important collectivity and affection are, and especially the value of family and friends. But they don't get lost in their ideas and thoughts, and are not easily influenced, but are determined and persistent in their search.

In a nutshell, this special young man I described in this chapter isn't a product of a mold in which the dough is put in and all the individuals come out the same, with no spark. We're talking about a set of skills that will allow this young man to achieve anything he wishes in life, be it in the personal or professional field.

We believe the role of the school and family is not to direct the child or the teenager, but to supply them with a set of values, knowledge, skills and feelings that allow them to overcome the obstacles of life that cast so many people aside, dealing with frustration and conformism. We shouldn't allow the same thing happen to them!

PSYCHOLOGICAL MATHEMATICS

Here I apologize again to the psychologists, psychiatrists, psychopedagogists and other professionals who study the human mind, for the simplification that I'll make here of important emotional processes which occur in the human mind. But, as previously stated, we are in an urgent regimen to change how the current schools deal (or don't deal) with the students' feelings. We must act quickly and a simplified vision may accelerate and facilitate things to the benefit of the students.

SELF-ESTEEM

Nobody enters a fight knowing they will lose!

A person with low self-esteem doesn't think they will lose. They know it for sure! And that's why they give up the fight even before they start. They don't take risks and, because they don't take risks, they don't win. And, when they don't win, they don't believe in themselves, and the vicious circle starts again, pushing their self-esteem further down.

This cycle turns the person into an easy target for opportunists, people who love to take care of those who don't believe in themselves, manipulating them as they like, leaving them increasingly unhappier for not allowing them to realize their wishes or express their opinions and feelings through their choices and behavior.

People with low self-esteem are weak, causing them to be consumed by envy, because they only find hope and consolation when those around them sink, coming down to their level, or even lower. And this confirms that that's life, there is no hope, they should accept that.

Others' success is something extremely painful for somebody with low self-esteem because it shows them all their weaknesses and, what may be worse, that there is a way out. But the way out passes through having faith in themselves, something that they will never have, because the pain of disillusion may be even more terrible. Better to keep things as they are.

On the other extreme, although a lot less common, we have people with extreme high self-esteem or those who think they are unbeatable, capable of everything, without limits.

Obviously in this case there is a high risk, not only regarding material and personal losses, but also a greater exposure to frustration. We know how much arrogance blinds people.

However, dear readers, I have to confess that, in my view, the number of people with excessively high self-esteem is hugely smaller than those with low self-esteem. We need to be careful with the low self-esteem covered by arrogance, i.e. those that snub so that they don't show who they really are.

Also, I believe that the losses from low self-esteem are a lot greater because they paralyze the person, preventing them from reacting. On the excessive side, life itself will provide for the necessary corrections. On the low self-esteem side, nothing can be done.

Thus, we have to feel powerful. We have to believe in ourselves, allow us to make mistakes, but especially, try.

We learn very little from mistakes, they teach us only one more way not to succeed. On the other hand, getting things right gives us a recipe for success. But mistakes are important, especially when we deal with them in a good way, as they are a demonstration of good self-esteem. Mistakes are made only by those who try, and only those who believe in themselves can try.

Therefore, it's important to teach students to deal with the frustrations of life without losing faith in themselves. They need to have a broad view of the world in order to allow their qualities and the difficulties that everybody has to face in order to achieve things. Therefore, they will not feel unable, they will realize that no great journey is without obstacles and that they will not be enough to prevent them to get what they wish.

FREEDOM

The concept of freedom is very broad. There are several approaches for this concept, and we can analyze it from a political, social, religious, personal, family-related point of view, amongst so many others. However, I'll concentrate the analysis on the concept of freedom by using a more personal approach. In this case, we'll take the meaning of freedom as a feeling, the "feel free" concept.

Self-esteem is not enough if the individual is not free from a series of evils, such as pressure from relatives, society and external models imported by the individual. I'll explain it better.

Imagine a young man who dreams to be an artist. However, unfortunately, his family have already mapped out his destiny as a doctor, following in his father's footsteps. After all, the father will not only guide his son in a successful career, but he also may open the doors to dozens of hospitals and clinics so that the young man may show his whole potential. But we're talking about a modern and wise family. They'll never make the young man follow a path determined by them. Instead, they'll be more democratic and will allow the young man to decide, but not without filling his head with all the possible and imaginable arguments that prove, without a shadow of doubt, how miserable he would be as an artist and extremely successful as an ear nose and throat specialist.

Was he given the freedom to choose? Will this young man really have an option? Well, if he's strong enough to keep firm in his purposes, he may overcome his family's pressure and follow his dream, but I wonder if during his childhood his parents taught him to resist external pressure and keep his convictions? Could a family who even decides the career of a young man have strengthened his self-esteem during his childhood? I wonder if he got to choose the clothes he wanted to wear to his friends' parties.

Freedom starts inside the person, but is determined by external agents: relatives, friends and teachers. It's not enough to believe in oneself and have a choice. Not if the person does not learn how to be free from several sources of pressure to which we're all subject to, including the opinion of friends and relatives, as well as the social model in which we are inserted. Several times we're completely against those who surround us, but we need to think that people around us don't feel the same as we and, therefore, may help, but must never decide for us.

The students must learn from a very early age, not only from their families, but also from their teachers, to follow their dreams and believe in their convictions. To be free to make their choices and assume the risks. How many Dalis, Picassos, and Warhols may have become frustrated doctors?

SELF-ESTEEM + FREEDOM = INDEPENDENCE

The person who believes that they may achieve things and has space for their achievements doesn't depend on anything else to make it happen.

Of course resources are still going to be necessary, but independent people may go after them on their own. We must remember João Guerreiro's story, previously told.

Freedom alone is not enough for a person to be independent. They may still depend on support, incentive, emotional support, help in taking personal decisions, amongst others, if they don't believe in themselves and take risks.

INDEPENDENCE + MOTIVATION = INITIATIVE

You cannot put your heart and soul into something you don't believe in or don't wish for.

Initiative comes from motivation, but is based on independence. Human beings need to believe that they can, then they have to let themselves go and wish to move along for something important to happen in their lives.

But we aren't talking about the initiative to call a client and close a new sale without consulting with your manager. We are talking here about having the initiative to change the course of one's life, to walk towards what is desired but uncertain. To roll up one's sleeves and build their happiness where, when and how one desires.

INITIATIVE + BASIC TOOLS = SUCCESS

Before anything else, I need to present my definition of success. In the meritocratic and capitalist society we live in, success equals money. It's common to hear things like: "She is successful, has an important position in a large corporation, lives in a luxury condominium, has dozens of servants in her home and travels by helicopter".

Is this a successful woman?

The answer is: it depends! Was this what she dreamt for her life? Was this the life style she longed for? She certainly paid, and still pays, a price to maintain a life style of a top executive. Does she think it's worthwhile? Is she happy with her life? If so, then she is a successful person.

Let's think about the young man of the previous example. If he becomes an important director of a large hospital, recognized and well compensated, would he have been successful? In my point of view, clearly not! His dream was to be an artist, his motivation was art, expression, creation, colors, forms and maybe something else that only he saw in the art. Is he pleased, or does he feel the burden of the "incredible" career he built for himself? And another question, more fundamental: would he have reached this success if each class in medical school was a sacrifice, or at least, boring?

Therefore, for me, success is to reach one's dreams, which could be to have a simple and happy family, to travel and live adventures throughout the world, to build an empire or even to write a book with the hope of gathering people interested in education for a happy life.

But how about the "basic tools"?

They form a set of knowledge and skills which allow students to perform any role they wish. For example: if they understand mathematics well, financial calculations may be easy for them. By developing the interpersonal communication, anyone will be able to make the necessary contacts in order to get good job opportunities. If they understand history, it will be easy for them to deal with different cultures, if they wish to travel the world. This is true for any field.

As it is impossible to foresee how much knowledge or what set of skills people will need in their lives, it's impossible to plan, in any subject, a deeper knowledge than what their skills indicate. However, the school and the parents must provide a "basic kit" to the children, which will be an important starting point for any journey they make during their lifetime.

Thus, with a good base of knowledge, skills and initiative to act, our students will be people that will look for their happiness by carrying out their own dreams, i.e., successful people.

Chapter III

WHAT TEACHERS (AND PARENTS) SHOULD DO

Let's be practical and see how we should deal with the students, especially children, in order to offer them everything we discussed previously, which will be the base of their success.

I'll describe below a series of important steps that teachers and parents must keep in mind during their daily contact with the children.

DON'T SEE A CHILD, SEE A HUMAN BEING

Few things irritate me more than this phrase: "Never mind! This is children's stuff. It'll go away!".

The child is a complete human being; he has feelings just like an adult. He has wishes, gets frustrated, excited, sad, hopeful, amongst the endless emotions human beings are able to feel.

Obviously, children have a more limited analysis and their feelings are less refined, but they feel with an intensity that sometimes may be greater than ours.

Do you remember how anxious you were the day before an important test at school? Were you less anxious than nowadays, before an important meeting at work?

Do you remember how frustrated you were when one of your aunts gave you a pair of black socks for your birthday? Is it different than the frustration you experience when you deliver a difficult report that took you days to prepare, being very careful about the data, and your boss answers: "put it there."

Children have feelings as well! For us, their situations seem silly and irrelevant, but for them, in the phase they're going through, they are very important.

Thus, one should see the child as a complete human being, respecting his feelings, in order to show that he is important, that his comments are relevant, i.e., that he is valuable. Or could his self-esteem be properly developed without this?

THINK AS A CHILD

There are several children that prefer to get clothes than toys on their birthdays or at Christmas, but to be honest, I've never met any.

In order to fully interact with a child, one needs to think as a child. To develop children is not to produce mini-adults, i.e. children who are precociously mature, who are prevented from having broad and continuous childhood phases. These children will become troubled adults, as we know how much childhood influences our adult life.

Children need to play, laugh, dream, be naughty, test adults, imagine, build, dismantle, and investigate. Adults need to respect their childhood. And never give a boy a pair of black socks (sorry I had to get that off my chest).

WHAT SEEMS TO BE UNIMPORTANT MAY BE VERY IMPORTANT!

One of the worst evils that children face in their lifetime is adults' lack of patience.

Sometimes, tasks that are simple for adults may be very complicated for a child, such as pouring milk from a carton into a mug, for example. How many mothers "go crazy" or "fall into a deep depression" when they see the child squeeze too much the carton or miss the mug and spill milk on the clean towel? They even shout at the child, who feels the most incompetent person on the planet because he cannot even manage to pour milk in the mug or feel guilty for causing so much suffering to his dear mother for such an appalling lack of ability.

What is more important here: the clean towel or the child's self-esteem? The 150 ml of spilt milk or the development of the child's motor coordination and initiative?

For the child, all that is as complicated a challenge as extracting the gross sales of the month in the company's new mysterious ERP system. Let's respect the children's stages of development!

IT'S FORBIDDEN TO TELL CHILDREN OFF

How to discipline children is an issue that always raises questions among parents and teachers, as many times they are lost and don't know how to act with more agitated or difficult children. How can we make them respect the rules without using aggressive methods?

At first, one needs to understand why aggression should not be used. Several parents believe that some slaps won't hurt. Some teachers end up by losing their temper and resort to shouting or using stronger words in order to remain in control of the situation.

Do you respect your superior because he is authoritarian?

When an adult shouts at a child, there are two possible outcomes: either no effect will be reached, except for more ill discipline, or he will reduce the child's self-esteem, even, possibly, causing trauma.

In the first case, children who disrespect rules will interpret the adults' lack of control as a demonstration of their power – the power of the children, not of the adults. As if they thought: "I'm so powerful that I make my father lose his temper! Look at him shouting like crazy! That's funny!." Therefore, the scolding starts softly and becomes intense over time. They simply show no authority.

When scolding reaches a higher level, becoming aggressive or even ending in a spanking, we have crossed a boundary that should never have been crossed: that of the disrespect of the child! A mother that spanks her child or a teacher that shouts at a student is taking something precious from the child, which is self-esteem. Therefore, they'll be raising children, and future adults, that are insecure and afraid of the world.

But how can we make more agitated children respect the rules? How do we keep the adult's authority without being aggressive?

Act-consequence. For everything we do in life, there is a consequence, positive or negative, that we must face. With children, it works the same way.

If the child keeps destroying his toys, he needs to lose the right to play with them. The adult must inform him in a clear manner: "If you keep breaking your toys, you'll only have the broken ones." If he continues, the adult must take all the good toys away and leave only those broken. But in a calm and serene manner, without showing any emotion to the child. The child's act was to break his toys, the consequence is to lose the right to play with the good toys.

Let's imagine a case in which a child is too aggressive with his classmates at school. This child must sit outside the circle as soon as he shows signs of aggression. He should remain isolated, but have visual contact with his friends and teacher, so he can feel the consequence of losing his friends (temporarily) for not treating them with respect. The teacher shouldn't show any emotion, but just inform the child that if he assaults his friends, he will lose the right to stay with them, as nobody there wants to get hurt. He may come back after reflecting and showing that he understood why he acted inappropriately, but not without first feeling the consequence of being set apart from his friends.

In these cases above, who took away the child's right to play with his toys or to take part in the activities with his friends? The mother? The teacher? No. It was the child! Thus, he really understands the reasons why he needs to behave, without feeling the need to become aggressive, which makes children even more impolite and insecure.

CHILDREN HAVE THE ANSWER

The main question a teacher has in the classroom is: "How am I supposed to teach them? How am going to make them learn?".

Unfortunately, there isn't one answer that is applicable to all classes, all children, and all places. There are more efficient methods, more efficient techniques, but even using them is no guarantee that all students will reach the expected results. But the good news is that the teacher may find out the small adjustments that must be made in his work so that the technique may be adjusted to each of his students, and only each student will be able to answer this.

It is key that teachers get in touch with their students, but never in a superficially manner. In order to be able to truly capture the best ways for each student, teachers need to donate themselves, to open their hearts so that the children can do the same (and they're so much better at this than us adults). Teachers must develop a connection with the students, and the only way to do that is via affection.

Not even the best psychologists may understand the emotions of a child if they don't feel whatever the child is feeling, if they don't put themselves in the child's shoes. Why do mothers know their children so well? Because they are completely and utterly connected to them. Though sometimes we see teachers that know their students better than the parents, but not because they spend more time with them, but because they care and get more involved with them.

Teachers should suffer over any defeat and vibrate with excitement over every victory their students achieve, the same way they would suffer and vibrate in their own defeats and victories. This is the only way to fully understand them and guide them in order that the students can know themselves in first place, so they can then discover the world.

SOLVE EVEN THE SMALLEST PROBLEMS BY THEMSELVES

Children must be educated with freedom. They need to try and solve their own problems; to try, fail and learn. Showing the result doesn't help to understand the learning process. The children need to learn how to learn, to find out that they can solve their own problems. This will create self-esteem, independence and initiative.

Don't do things for your students or children, help them to find out how they can do it for themselves. Show that you believe in them, and that they can believe in themselves.

This rule should be applied from putting the lid back on the bottle until solving a Physics problem.

If you believe in them, they will believe in themselves as well.

FIND THEIR OWN QUESTIONS

For the children to develop their self-esteem, independence and initiative, adults must not give the answers, but help them to find the answers for themselves. We don't have ready answers in life, we need to find them by ourselves.

But even more important than finding their own answers, is to find their own questions. This task is extremely difficult and us adults are not prepared to find them, which makes it even harder to build happiness.

What are your dreams? What do you like? What would you like to change in your life? How can you improve in your relationships? Do you want to improve them?

How frequently do people ask themselves these questions? It shouldn't be difficult to maintain a good level of reflection about your own life. Being aware of who we are and what we want is half the journey to happiness.

Children must be stimulated to look for their answers and, especially, their questions since from an early age, so that they're always open to themselves. So that they know themselves and go after their own dreams, which may never be reached if they don't know, at least, what those dreams are.

Who are we? Where are we going? These questions generate

individual answers and that must be answered only by the person themselves, via a self-awareness process and personal choices.

Life has the meaning we decide to give it.

PEDAGOGY IS A PRIORITY

Every problem, every discussion, every curiosity and every need are learning opportunities. Teachers need to have more freedom to develop the contents according to the students' interests and invest more time in seemingly minor aspects, giving way to children's curiosities and interests.

Schools put too many limits on the teacher's work. Everything is preformatted, preplanned, predefined and, what is worse, predigested! What can we expect from this? A limited result, of course, as, besides discouraging both teachers and students, schools don't allow them to travel through knowledge and discover the world and life.

Also, too much time is wasted with lesson plans, evaluation, attendance control, reports, schedules, daily planners and all the other "bureaucratic" tasks, while the time with the students is reduced.

Principals, get rid of the bureaucracy and release your students and teachers! Imagine and create with them! Education is a wonderful trip of discovery. Embark on it as well.

WALKING METAMORPHOSIS

As I consider myself a "lifelike" person, I cannot consider the education we adopt today at "Escola do Max" as a definitive solution. Life changes all the time. The life we live today is very different from that of our parents and grandparents. Education must follow life and its changes.

Schools must adjust their techniques and contents to what life will require from their students in the future, not today. Programs must be defined based on what is the trend today.

Thus, it's impossible to think that any one education proposal is the best. It may be the best for a certain community at a certain time. Tomorrow, things could be completely different.

The changes also come to make improvements. Schools cannot be afraid of trying, making mistakes, changing and learning. This is the only way to get an on-going evolution.

Be a walking metamorphosis and change your mind completely at any time. This is a sign of courage and intelligence.

THE CHILD AS AN ACTIVE AGENT OF THE PROCESS

A lot has been said about the change in the teachers' role as a more passive agent in the teaching-learning process, while the child becomes an active agent. But I haven't seen this being put into practice. In fact, what I have seen are pseudoconstructivist proposals which limit the whole area of exploration for the children, leaving little space for them to navigate through knowledge. How is it possible for children to build their own knowledge if they are not even allowed to choose the tools?

For the children to be really active agents in the process, they must have the power to choose, to question, to answer, to evaluate, to correct, to try again, to learn.

QUESTIONS AND ANSWERS

Children must seek their answers by themselves. They should be educated to learn how to use the necessary tools to obtain the information they need, either by using books, magazines, the internet, interviewing people outside the school, scientific experiments conducted by them, movies, amongst so many other sources of information. Learning how to use these resources, children can look for their own answers.

But this is nothing new. What may be new is that, besides looking for their answers, children must learn to look for their own questions.

What should I know in order to be able to do a certain thing? What do I need to learn in order to build a rocket that really flies? What do I want to achieve? What do I want for my life? Should I marry this person? Should I change jobs?

Learning how to ask the right questions is usually more important than finding the right answer.

Teachers must look to develop citizens that don't follow the crowd, but that are capable of questioning and reflecting.

EVALUATION

Children must develop their own evaluation, not only of their performance, but also of the method used and activities proposed.

At "Escola do Max," we work with projects that have a final activity, chosen by the students. Amongst other advantages, this methodology allows students to monitor their own evolution of knowledge, as, in order to reach the proposed goals, they need to solve a series of actual problems, which put them in contact with pedagogical goals.

The students may, and should, be active agents even of their own evaluation, as in life they won't have somebody at their side to tell them how much they got right or wrong. They will need to realize for themselves where they should improve in order to become closer to their goals.

Of course the teacher will also make an evaluation. But this task will be shared with the students, so that they understand, in general lines, what they need to learn.

As a suggestion, I believe that the best way to do so at the moment is via an on-going evaluation based on the teacher's observation, but in a way that the children know what the main and most important criteria are.

THE TEACHERS' IDEAL ROLE

In order for their students to be prepared for life (and through it), teachers must change their attitude from "teaching" to:

I. ADOPTING AN OBSERVER APPROACH
Students must solve their own problems, the teacher must be more of an observer than an agent in the process.

2. MOTIVATING
Teachers must give emotional support to their students so that they move forward, so that they fight and overcome their challenges.

3. GUIDING
Teachers must help the students whenever they are lost, showing possible ways to move forward.

4. STIMULATING
Teachers must be a source of stimuli, sending out messages that raise feelings in the students and several types of answers that take them in different directions. With that, the students will find something to be explored not only in the world, but within themselves as well.

5. CHALLENGING

Teachers must push them forward to overcome their limits, as well as provoke them to show that they can trust themselves.

6. COLLABORATING

Working together with the students, but as another member of the team, never as a leader.

7. FACILITATING

Certain passages don't need to offer their whole level of difficulty. Teachers must step in when a difficulty arises that is improper for the students' stage, becoming an obstacle in their progress.

8. ALLOWING THEM TO MAKE MISTAKES

Contrary to common thinking, we don't learn a lot from our mistakes. They are only another way to not reach the expected result. When we do things right, then we learn a lot. They clearly show what should be done in order to reach our goals. However, making mistake means freedom. The students' mistakes must be valued as a demonstration of an attempt, of their self-esteem, of believing in themselves, of allowing themselves to do things, to not mind what others think or say. Mistakes are an exercise of freedom. Only those who try can get it right, and only those who believe that they will get it right can try. Therefore, we should let our students make mistakes and have fun with them.

Chapter IV

"LIFELIKE" PROJECTS

Up until now, the more skeptical reader will be asking: "Right. This is all very nice, but how can all this ideology be applied in the classroom?".

We don't live in an ideal world, and of course it has several problems that limit the application of this whole ideology. Amongst them, we have the teachers' resistance to changes, principals with a limited view, mistrusting parents, and even legal limitations imposed by the Ministry of Education.

The interesting part is that I'm not including the students amongst the factors which make it difficult to apply the ideology. In fact, I have noticed that quite the contrary: the student ends up being the facilitator in the whole implementation of pedagogic projects based on concepts connected to the "lifelike" approach. The huge interest shown by them regarding the activities proposed (by themselves) transcends the classroom, and several parents come and talk to me, due to their surprise at having noticed that their children continue to research and explore at home the themes worked on in the classroom. Thus, we manage to get a huge reduction in the mistrust of the parents, as it ends together with the principal's limited view, when the students' excitement converts into positive results in the evaluations. The students who are actively involved in the process produce more, better and faster. Their growth is surprising and the only party that isn't happy is the government, which insists in laws, decrees, directives and rules that have been outdated for decades, limiting and preventing the school from evolving, following the changes seen in our society.

Thus, at "Escola do Max," we allowed our students to show to our whole community that a "lifelike" approach is possible and that we managed to develop our own methodology based fully on the ideology presented in the previous chapters.

The term "Lifelike Projects," which we use to name our methodology, comes from using education via projects in order to implement actual ideas and enterprises so that students may experience actual problems and situations. In other words, to open the classroom's doors so that life can get in. Therefore, the students will learn for life and via life.

SOME WORDS ABOUT THE PROJECTS

A lot has been written, talked and invented about teaching via projects. Several schools have been incorporating this way of teaching to their pedagogical planning. Each one in their own way, we can see projects being used, from small initiatives that get the whole school involved on a special date, until bolder schools which have decided to use this technique as a base for every pedagogical decision in the school environment.

When I was a student, in the nostalgic decade of the 80's, I remember being extremely excited over the possibility of making something different in the Science Fairs or Cultural Weeks. They were my opportunities to explore the world of science with dazzling projects. I waited the whole year for those rare occasions when I would be able to go beyond books and make something really interesting.

In a certain year, we had the pedagogical coordinator in our room, who proudly came to invite the students to prepare projects to present to parents and guests at another Science Fair. I clearly remember how happy I felt when she introduced the subject, speaking about the Fair, and I remember even clearer how frustrated I felt when she informed us that the "only" restriction was that any project would have to involve a specific theme: the FIFA's World Cup. "This isn't fair!," I thought. "I don't like soccer" and considering my lack of talent for the game, it was just as well. So this was how our pedagogical coordinator just dashed my hopes and made it impossible for me to pursue about ten science projects I already had in mind.

Of course many of my colleagues loved the theme, especially those who felt connected to the sport. This until they found out that they would do everything in that project, except for playing ball.

I'm mentioning an example of my own life because we need to show that, even creating very well structured and elaborated projects, that go beyond the frontiers of the classroom, that involve the whole school, even so, not much would have been achieved, except for a new package for knowledge. In order for the students to really learn, they need to be involved, body and soul, with the project, but they won't be able to do that without noticing a real purpose to the whole thing and that it is something that motivates them.

More (un)interesting projects

My frustration was so great mainly because that would be one of the rare opportunities that I would have to go beyond the books, exercise lists and tests, elements which comprised the methodology of the school where I studied during the whole elementary, middle and high school. Nowadays, there are many approaches via projects which are less conservative and offer their students greater opportunities to realize, and even experience, how knowledge can be applied via projects offered by the school, which are carried out very frequently and in a great variety.

By building a normal sized house, using recyclable materials, a teacher can teach his students important concepts of mathematics (in the geometrical division of the rooms), geography (exploring social issues in the different types of houses), sciences (showing how important recyclability is and its impact on the environment), amongst others. Some schools are preparing several projects like this, so that the students can visualize all knowledge through practice. This approach avoids students becoming frustrated, as they don't feel stuck with books, annotations, exercises in notebooks and empty debates in the classroom. However, I'd like to ask: In this type of modern and interesting approach how much are the students involved in the decision-making process, especially regarding choosing the project?

"Teacher, we prefer to build a car instead of a house. Is it possible?"

And the teacher thinks: "But I spent the whole weekend getting ready to build a house!"

This occurs because the teacher created a simulation of the reality, and didn't allow life to enter the classroom. Her students didn't have the opportunity to make decisions, to assume risks with different ideas, to open themselves up to new possibilities. She has tried to control the development of things, but life doesn't work that way, causing her students to become frustrated.

STUDENTS SHOULD CHOOSE

How can we get the students to become interested in the learning process?

"Teachers don't teach, students learn." We are tired of hearing this old saying. However, for me, it's only half true.

The students are those who learn. Without a doubt, if the students decide not to learn, there is only one alternative: go back to the old traditional model and, through a lot of pressure and below-average grades, force them to convince us, who in our turn, pretend to believe that they have learnt something. But, in fact, they cheated or learnt by heart whatever we would like to see in their answers, even being fully aware that the right answer there doesn't mean that they have learnt the concept and can apply it to another situation.

"Teachers don't teach." This is the false part, and even makes the old saying stupid. Teachers who think they can't teach if the students don't want to learn are portraying themselves as weak and lazy. The magic of education is to seduce the students with the beauty of knowledge and life. But it's no good imagining that they will take to trigonometry with the same enthusiasm as a Mathematics teacher if, in the first place, they would prefer to be anywhere else than in a classroom with 20, 30 or 50 other students, quiet and "concentrated" with the "master" who "conducts" all the "teaching" (yes, I meant the inverted commas).

Secondly, the old classic indignation of most of the (dull) students: "What should I learn this for?"

Using projects help a lot in this last aspect, as it shows the students that the knowledge transmitted by the teacher is really useful for their real life. But this doesn't solve the whole problem of keeping students interested.

So, in order for the students to be involved body and soul (and not just the body) in the classes, projects, debates, or in any activity, the following are necessary:

1. Motivation (the student needs to want to perform the activity)
2. Meaning (the student needs to understand why that activity is being performed)

Imagine if all students understood the relevance of the subject discussed and, even more, if they were excited about the theme and wanted more and more. Wouldn't classes be a success?

So, by using projects, but in a dynamic and "lifelike" manner, in which the students are the center of the decision making in the classroom and there is a search for real life situations, we manage to get exactly this result. That is to say, by letting the students choose what and how to study, the methodology via the "Lifelike Projects," developed by us at "Escola do Max," has been offering exactly the two aspects above, pushing the learning process forward, and greatly increasing the results achieved.

This new approach of working with projects, which we will describe in detail further on, is the result of around three years of research, including an extensive bibliographical search for new approaches that would put the students at the center of the decision making process in the classroom. Invaded by the frustration of not finding any reference of this type, we invested many hours in meticulous observation of the children, which included a lot of practical research and the development of a new approach that would really achieve the goals that we sought: the perception, on the part of the students, of the meaning of the knowledge by experimenting with real situations and problems, where they could use the knowledge; and the motivation of learning how to use the knowledge to reach results defined by the students themselves (motivation and meaning, based on real life).

The approach via the "Lifelike Projects" was developed for preschoolers and first years students in elementary school, but with some adaptations it can be implemented also for older students in elementary school and even high school students. Surprisingly, we see a special potential of this approach for the post-secondary school. However, the application of the "Lifelike Projects" in these levels will be the object of a further study, allowing for new publications.

Commentaries from readers will be very much appreciated, so that our approach may be questioned and tested thoroughly, allowing for its development to continue and reach even better results with new contributions.

The methodology through "Lifelike Projects" should also be a walking metamorphosis, so that its evolution follows the evolution of those who believe that life must be an inspiration, a theme and a goal.

Chapter V

THE METHODOLOGY STEP-BY-STEP

Now, I'll explain how a "Lifelike Project" is developed, by using a step-by-step method. It's worth noting that, by adopting a "lifelike" ideology, there is no control over what is to be studied or built or developed by the children. In fact, we have noticed that, whenever a teacher tries to take the students towards a subject or goal, usually the whole range of situations to be experienced disappears, as there is no longer any direct interest from the students, as well as all the desired psychological reactions when the students decide and accept the consequences and difficulties that their choices generate.

However, a methodology and certain limits are necessary, otherwise it would be as if the learning process would occur by magic just by leaving the students to their own devices. Thus, there is a series of steps, activities and procedures to be followed in order for the students to create and develop appropriate situations, though real, to experience the contents to be developed.

Each lifelike project follows the same sequence of steps, each with well defined objectives, as seen below:

PHASE I – CHOOSING THE THEME
Exposure
Brainstorming
Voting

PHASE II – EXPLORING THE THEME
Preparing the Map
Initial research
Choosing the Final Project

PHASE III - ENTERPRISE
Development
Final Project

Though the duration of each step is subject to the students' decisions, we recommend certain limits of duration, so that the global benefit from the project is the best possible. The step 7 (development) is an exception, and its duration may vary enormously, depending on the students' interests and decisions.

Our experience has shown that, for the project to yield its best results, its duration must be coordinated with the students in order that it doesn't last less than 2 or 3 weeks, the minimum time necessary for the theme and the students' ideas to be extensively explored, and never more than 2 months, depending on the theme, the students' interest and how complex the final project is. Above this period, we start to compromise other pedagogical objectives which haven't been contemplated by the project, as it will generate situations allowing contents specific to that project to be experienced.

PHASE I – CHOOSING THE THEME

As previously explained, for a successful learning process, the students need to be motivated to study the subject, and the easiest way to achieve that is to let them choose the subject they would like to study.

This idea may seem absurd, because if they don't choose the subject that the teacher needs to teach, it won't be covered. False! The first thing that one must have in mind is that in the approach via Lifelike Projects, there is not a sequence of themes to be covered, each subject will be presented in its own time, according to the needs of each project.

Let's think how human beings gained their knowledge about the world. We invented the wheel in order to carry all the necessary weight, we discovered agriculture so that we didn't need to depend on our luck in finding food, we invented electric power to illuminate our homes in a more efficient, economic and practical manner than that offered by candles, and so on and so forth. Each discovery or invention was due to human necessity, in order to have a safer and more pleasant environment, or to understand the universe surrounding us. The world and life don't come with instructions, we need to find them.

So it is our approach. The students are pushed by their own desires, therefore having problems, needs or even curiosities, and in order to overcome them, the students will need knowledge that they will have to develop by themselves. As previously discussed, in this ideology, the students look for their own answers, and also for their own questions. They ask themselves what they want to reach, how they will achieve their goals and then they go after the necessary knowledge and skills in order to do that.

Therefore, the teacher doesn't choose the theme for the classes. The theme comes naturally through the decisions of the students, especially in choosing the final project and the theme of the project.

STEP I - EXPOSURE

When this methodology was being developed, we tried several times to start the projects via brainstorming, in which each student freely contributed with his suggestions for themes. We always faced the same problem: the themes suggested were about the latest toys, movies or TV characters, games or objects in the classroom. We need to consider that we're dealing with preschoolers and students in the first years of elementary school.

Although these themes have generated interesting projects, they didn't have all the educational potential necessary for a truly efficient project. Also, the themes were often repeated between classes, some times even in the same class.

Another important observation deals with the limited character of the children's universe. I say that with absolute conviction: our children are exposed to an incredibly limited and limiting universe! If the readers are already surprised by a child's imagination, then they should see our students, whose universe expanded beyond the high fences of the main media, books, cartoons, toys, etc. Children healthily exposed to the real world, to the beauty of our planet, to the exciting history of Humanity, and the endless wonders of life can be incredibly imaginative, even showing great command of the world surrounding them, an effect that not even the best cartoon studios would be able to reproduce.

In order to knock the castle walls down and free our children from their limited universe, we created the present stage of exposure: during around 20 minutes, the children look and explore a kit of several materials, comprised of magazines and books with different themes. From magazines about cars to computer programming, from life in the countryside to the academic world, even fashion magazines must be used, as you never know where the idea for the next project will come from. The materials must be rich in photos and, therefore, magazines are best. Here I need to add one thing: the teacher must check each piece of material beforehand, in order to avoid exposing the children to violent images, adult content or sensual images, among other themes that are improper for them.

The students must be encouraged to look for images that arise their curiosity, things which they would like to study about or experience. This incentive is key for them to perceive more themes and suggest themes that transport them to places beyond their limited child's universe.

When implementing this technique in the classroom, the reader will realize that the characters, toys and idols are completely cast aside when the students find the universe of possibilities in the materials. As children are free to choose themes even if they are not in the magazines, their favorite characters, toys and idols keep being listed in the suggestions, though this is rare, and they are rarely voted on.

This step continues with the students flipping through the magazines, and talking about the themes which interest them.

The children explore diverse materials in order to choose the theme of the project.

STEP 2 - BRAINSTORMING

Still with the magazines in their hands, the students suggest themes for the project that may be listed in several ways, according to each class and teacher.

Depending on the level of literacy of the class, each student may write their own idea directly on the blackboard or on an activity sheet. If the class is still not ready for that, the teacher may write each student's idea on the board.

In this step, it's very important that the teacher gives no opinion or comment in order to not influence the students' opinions, as they must make their own suggestions following their own wishes. Teachers should also control those students that show more leadership, so that they don't take away their colleagues' right to choose.

Besides the themes gathered in the magazines, the students may also suggest themes that haven't been chosen in previous opportunities or in which they are personally interested.

The children suggest the themes of their interest and the teacher writes them down on the board.

I must warn the reader at this point to carefully analyze those ideas that, many times, "come from home." We've seen many cases in which the parents tried to influence the children to specific themes in order to create opportunities such as field trips to interesting places. If you see a similar case, ask the child for further details and whether the desire is really his or his family's.

Each child must be free to choose his theme!

STEP 3 - VOTING

With a list of all the suggested themes, the teacher gathers all the materials and starts a debate about each idea. The author of each one may start, presenting the positive points of his idea, trying to get their friends' votes. Everyone must be encouraged to present their opinions about each theme.

Contrary to adults, children quickly learn that they may not vote for their own themes, being open in choosing the most interesting idea, regardless of who provided the idea. Despite this, there may be cases in which a child tries to approve a certain theme in several voting sessions and never get it approved or, even with varied themes, his ideas never find support. For these cases, the teacher may do two things: explain that we don't always get what we want at the time we want, preparing the child to deal with his frustration, or ask his friends to collaborate in order to give their friend's ideas a chance, as he is persistently putting them to a vote. This last action should be avoided, but adopted in case of great frustrations, when the child tries several times to approve a project throughout the school year.

The voting per se may be carried out in ballots, or with each child voting in his favorite option among those listed on the board, or by asking their positive or negative vote to each idea. One must be really careful to choose the proper technique for each class, in order to avoid, for example, everyone following and voting for their best friend's theme.

The children must be able to conduct the process by themselves as much as possible, which includes counting the votes at the end.

When the project's theme has been chosen, the teacher must pay attention to the students that were frustrated for not having their themes chosen, trying to show them that the chosen project also has positive points, and that other opportunities for other projects will come up in the future. Frustration is part of life, things don't always work out the way we want, so we must teach our students to persevere and have patience, showing them that there is always a next time. In some cases, we must accept defeat.

Knowing how to deal with frustration is an important phase for human development, which will be very important for them in becoming mature adults.

The voting is done by the children's acceptance or not of the idea.

PHASE II – EXPLORING THE THEME

The previous phase's objective is to prepare the children to choose their project's theme. In this phase, we intend to put them in touch with the chosen theme, so that they can get a minimum repertoire allowing them to define the final project, or the project's main goal, from their point of view.

STEP 4 – PREPARING THE MAP

The map of the project is a registration of all questions and hypotheses presented by the children about the project's theme. In this step, the teacher may request the students to list everything they would like to know about the theme or aspects they think they already know. If the theme of the project is "Tyrannosaurus Rex," the students may suppose that the Tyrannosaurus Rex may be found at the zoo. It doesn't matter whether the statement is false; the teacher must leave the hypotheses to be confirmed or denied during the development of the project. A student may also ask: "Is the Tyrannosaurus Rex taller than my father?." Again, the answer will be provided by the project. The teacher must never answer, but only help the students to find the answers. It would be even interesting to invite the said father to visit the school, so that the class can measure his height and compare with what they researched in books, magazines or the internet to answer who is the tallest. Every experiment adds to the learning experience.

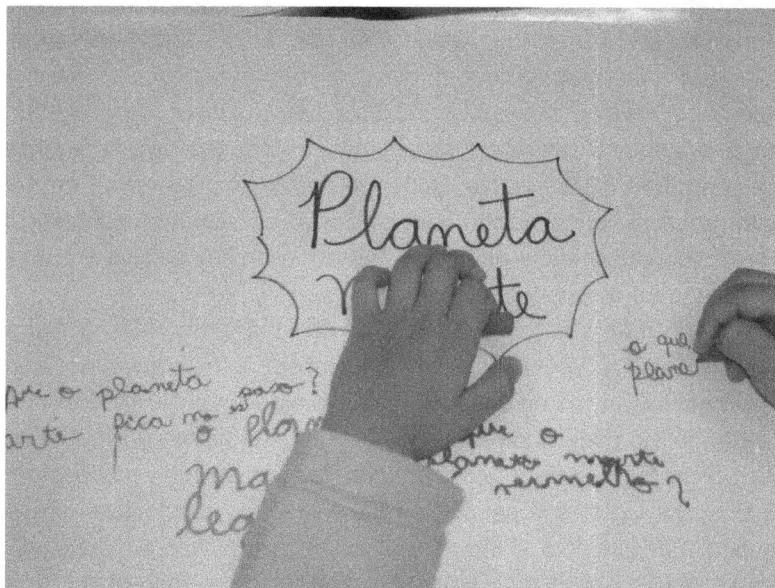

The children register what they know and what they want to know about the theme.

Currently, at "Escola do Max," the map of the project is made on a card, where the students themselves or the teacher, depending on the class' literacy stage, write the theme of the project in the middle and distribute all the answers and hypotheses around the theme. Then the board is fixed to the classroom wall and is checked throughout the whole project, especially at the initial stages, adding new questions, answers or simply reviewing some information.

Step 5 – Initial research

The map of the project is like a list of the tasks from the stage of the initial research. The teacher indicates each question raised by the students and questions them where they might find the answers – let's remember that the map lists the questions and hypotheses raised by the students themselves, the teacher here only helps them to organize their ideas and tasks. The students usually suggest the computer (the internet) or asking someone directly, amongst others. We should let them try to find their answers by themselves, so that they can develop autonomy and initiative. However, it's important to provoke them regarding the source's trustworthiness, in order to develop their critical sense. Does the author of the website on the internet really understand about dinosaurs? Does the secretary in the school really know whether a Tyrannosaur Rex is taller than the father of one of the students?

The theme is explored by following the project's map, but it doesn't need to be stuck to it. During research, new questions and hypotheses may come up, that may be explored by the students and added to the map. Endless curiosities and subthemes will come up and, with them, several opportunities for the learning process not only about the theme per se, but the pedagogical objectives of the school. For example, during the research about dinosaurs, the students may develop their writing/reading skills, reading small texts extracted from the internet, of specialized books or magazines. The student's objective is to extract the answer for his question, but the teacher must use the process to pass along further knowledge.

For this step, two to five days are suggested, which may be extended depending upon the student's interest and the amount of questions and hypotheses related to the project's map.

Through the computer, children search the answer for their own doubts.

STEP 6 – CHOOSING THE FINAL PROJECT

At the end of the initial research, the students already know enough regarding the theme in order to define what they want to achieve with the project. This is a very important moment, and it's the only occasion in which the teacher may influence the children's choices, in order to provoke and challenge, but never to guide.

Studying the Tyrannosaurus Rex, the students may decide to visit a museum where there is a skeleton of a Tyrannosaurus Rex. If the theme is Paris, they will want to visit it (I'll tell you what to do in this case). Building a pyramid could be the conclusion of a project about Egypt and so forth.

The students suggest the activities they like and then they vote to decide which is the best.

The teacher's influence, in this case, should aim at avoiding weak final projects, which could greatly reduce the learning experience. For example, if the children are very excited about studying sharks, to produce a poster to put in the corridor may not be the most appropriate final project. However, producing a video to send to parents and family members, preparing a theatrical play, visiting an aquarium, building a life-size shark may be more interesting both for the students, who will experience more challenging situations, and for the teacher, who needs more opportunities for the teaching-learning process. Thus, the process of deciding the final project must be another debate among the students, with the teacher taking part by provoking the students to think and, depending on the case, suggesting improvements to their ideas. What the teacher may never do is to sell a finished idea to the children. This could completely ruin the project, as it strongly depends on the children's desire to participate.

Over time, and with the practice acquired after participating in several lifelike projects, the children become increasingly more critical and articulate, to the point of sabotaging any idea that they don't find interesting. They create a situation that is, at the same time, frustrating and exciting, showing that they can really assume control on the work, getting involved body and soul.

Thus, the teacher must provoke and challenge, never convince. In practice: "What I understood is that you want to show everyone what you've learnt about sharks. Is that correct? But will a poster be enough to show everything we've learnt?," or still, "And now that we already know a lot of things regarding Paris, what are we going to do with everything we've learnt?." Another way: "What will be our final project for our 'Egypt' project?."

Choosing the final project is so important because 80 to 90% of the project is, in fact, a succession of tasks in order to perform the final project. It's while performing these tasks that the teacher will find the teaching opportunities that he needs to comply with his role.

The final project is the project's final goal, which the students intend to reach having completed the initial research. As the final project usually is more complex - an aspect that must be encouraged by the teacher -, the students must perform a series of activities and experiments, check sources of information and solve real problems. This will take them to complete the final project they so much look forward to, besides learning the several disciplines along the way, be they Mathematics, Portuguese, Science, Geography, History, Entrepreneurism, Communication, among all the other disciplines required or not by the government. Next we'll see how this process occurs.

PHASE III - ENTERPRISE

This is the phase in which the project really happens. We can understand the two previous phases as a preparation for the enterprise phase. From this point onwards, the children have a clear view of what they want to achieve and they are open to develop any necessary activity in order to make their idea real, i.e., that their final project is carried out.

STEP 7 - DEVELOPMENT

The teacher reviews with the children what they want to achieve and helps them to analyze the steps to be taken. Depending on each idea, the children will prepare budgets, schedules, lists of tasks, lists of materials, among other instruments to plan their activities.

For example, if the final project decided by them is a visit to the city's aquarium to see a shark up close, they have to define the field trip's date, get the necessary authorization, negotiate transportation, gather the necessary amount of money, etc. This last aspect generates endless opportunities to stimulate the children's entrepreneurism. We have lost count of how many times we have been offered to buy cakes, popcorn or pies, not including the times children have surprised me by requesting loans to fund their businesses, such as a paid theater presentation, recording CDs or even negotiating the execution of some task in the school, as a temporary job, serving their classmates in the refectory, for example.

Each need generates a teaching opportunity. In order to prepare the budget for a field trip, the children will need to know the currency of their country, learn to count, add, subtract, divide and multiply. Each step at the right time, the teacher simplifies each activity so that the necessary learning process occurs, adequate to each age. Thus, with distinct levels of complexity, all classes will calculate their budgets.

The lists generate special opportunities to develop writing/reading skills. From lists of tasks to lists of materials, this type of activity allows for a sound approach dedicated to literacy.

The teacher must take care of some aspects while implementing the activities. The teacher must never create a situation or implement an activity that isn't a genuine necessity of the project. Otherwise, the students will go back to that old question: "Why do I have to learn (or do) this?". With a genuine need, this question doesn't arise. "Ah! I have to learn to write in order to be able to send the authorization request so that my mother can let me go to the aquarium."

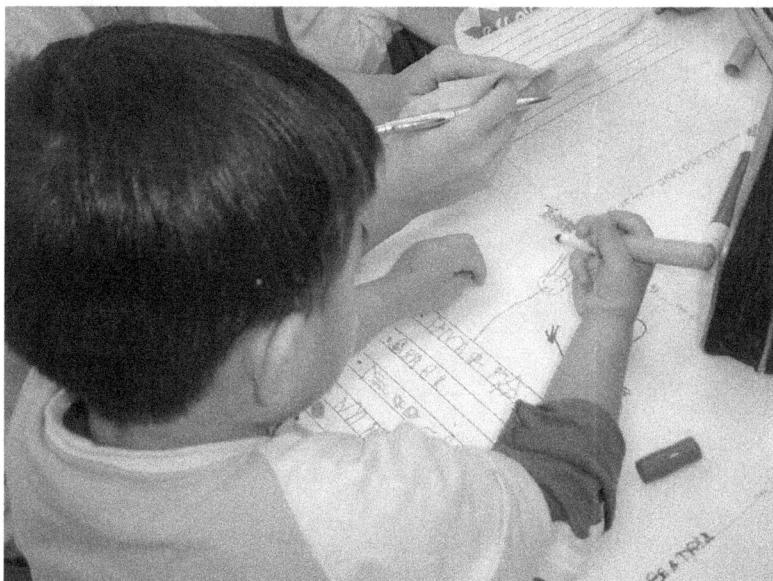

A four-year-old child writes the list of the materials needed for the conclusion activity.

Therefore, the students want to perform all activities as early as possible so that they can make their ideas real, which is the final project. Besides understanding the need for learning at each step of the process (motivation and meaning), the anxiety generated by the excitement with the enterprise itself makes them concentrate and be fully dedicated to the activities proposed. We again highlight that this will only occur if they are genuine needs of the project. Children are very clever and they soon realize any attempt by the teacher to direct them to a teaching purpose, which for them is purposeless, clearly conducted by the teacher, and not for the accomplishment of their final project which, for them, is the reason why they are all there.

The reader could raise the question about the validity of this situation, after all it is good to learn and the children's taste for learning must be awakened. So, I'll answer with another question: does the reader already fully know how the parts of your car work? Besides being interesting, this knowledge would be very useful in case of car trouble, right?

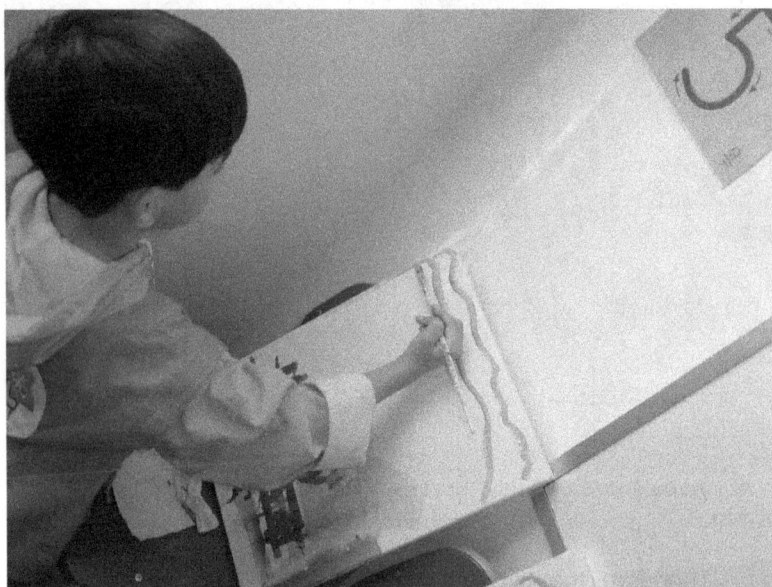

In order to have the conclusion activity made and, therefore, to have a painting, the children went through many stages: they've chosen the materials, asked for them, bought them and, in the end, painted it.

Of course learning is motivating per se, but we want to learn things that interest us, that will be useful or necessary for us. Children operate in the same way: they will enjoy learning, but only those things that are necessary or interesting for them, from their child's point view. Thus, the final project joins "business with pleasure" and directs the children towards knowledge. And I can assure you that the excitement they feel about their discoveries when they are in control is enviable.

The same occurs with reading. Developing the love for reading is possible only when there is freedom to read whatever one wants, a situation which occurs all the time, as the children are always reading contents which belong to the theme of the projects they have chosen.

STEP 8 – FINAL PROJECT

The end of the lifelike project occurs with the completion of the final project, whether it is a play, a visit to the aquarium, an exhibition of the pyramid that was built or any other idea presented and voted upon by the students.

To conclude a project about soccer, there is nothing better than visiting Pacaembu.

The completed final project must be celebrated with the children, who should receive as much positive feedback as possible. After all, that is the result of a great and long effort that involved everyone, culminating in a moment of joy and celebration of the success obtained. Remembering that in our lifelike approach, success means when our own dreams are reached, putting aside any family or socio-capitalist model. The children's dream at that time is being reached, and that's why they are successful.

Children must learn an important lesson, which should be conducted by the teacher, at the end of the final project: you can achieve almost anything in life with effort and dedication, and children have everything they need to make their dreams come true, and they should always believe in themselves, joining strength, determination and persistency. A good talk and a retrospect of the project is enough to consolidate these aspects.

IMPOSSIBLE FINAL PROJECTS

But how about when children decide to do something impossible or not feasible? For these occasions, it's very important that the teacher:

I. DOES NOT TELL THE CHILDREN DIRECTLY THAT THEIR IDEA IS NOT FEASIBLE

Children will understand that as a prohibition or unwillingness. They won't perceive that their idea is not feasible and, most of the time, they will only think: "We can't go to Paris because the teacher said we have no money." But deep down, the children are wondering about how much their pocket money will add up.

Thus, the children should realize themselves that their idea is not feasible, within an adequate rhythm and intensity, therefore avoiding significant shocks of frustration.

The project should be carried out as usual, considering the final project to be feasible. This includes checking the prices of tickets to Paris and the availability of seats on the flight and rooms in the hotel.

2. DON'T STIMULATE THE CHILDREN'S EXCITEMENT

The more excited they are, the more frustrated they will be when they discover that their idea is not feasible.

The teacher must, little by little, start to make them reluctant about their idea, raising problems so that they think about the solution. In time, they will test their concepts and start seeing the facts.

"I wonder if we'll have enough money to buy the tickets? I heard they are very expensive!" Or even: "When I was a child, my mother didn't let me travel by myself."

3. BE CAREFUL AT THE TIME OF TRUTH

The moment when they realize that their project is impossible is a very delicate one, and the teacher must be careful. He must put himself in the children's situation and help them overcome frustration.

"We can't go to Paris now, because you're children, but when you grow older, you'll be able to go." Or, "when you're adults and have a job, you'll be able to save money to go to Paris". "We can't go to Paris, but can't we do something else?".

The intention here is that they learn to deal with frustration in a positive manner, looking for other ways to face the situation, which includes accepting the fact, but also adapting to the new reality. They can't go to Paris, but maybe Paris can come to them? Children always find alternatives for these situations very quickly and efficiently when the teacher transmits support and optimism.

WEAK THEMES AND PROJECTS

A weak project is a project that doesn't have the children's adhesion. Even with all the freedom of choice and the teacher's support, sometimes the children choose a theme that doesn't generate the necessary interest for a good evolution, especially at the beginning of the year, in classes that are still not used to working with lifelike projects.

Usually, the reasons for that are laziness, ill discipline, interest for another event or object, like a toy brought by a friend, for example. The teacher must avoid choosing and voting on themes on those days in which the children are less concentrated or more agitated. If the teacher insists, the whole work may be lost on the following days, when the students won't have an active participation in any activity within the theme.

However, in certain cases, especially in cases of ill discipline, the teacher must continue with the project regardless, but with a reduced duration. What could be done in a month should be done within a week, only to show the children that they should be very careful in choosing their themes, as their decision will reflect in the group's future activities. Our experience shows that they learn really fast, and show great concern in the next voting sessions. Therefore, we recommend that all projects have start, middle and end, never being interrupted without a conclusion. The students need to learn to finish the processes they start.

RECORDING ACTIVITIES AND REPORTS

The approach through Lifelike Projects tries to extend the horizons of action and construction of the children beyond a sheet of paper, allowing them to express themselves through concrete constructions, presentations using their own bodies, events, among others. However, the activities on paper have extreme pedagogical relevance, so that they are encouraged and used, but without being mandatory regarding amount and frequency, always following the project's needs. Thus, if it's necessary to prepare an authorization request for the parents, paper is needed; this is also valid if a budget is necessary. However, if the students prefer to make a sculpture instead of a drawing, no recommendation is made for recording on paper. The project's needs establish when a record will be made.

However, most parents (and many principals) want to see what a child is doing at school and miss paper material (a legacy from the traditional learning process). In order to meet this desire, at "Escola do Max," we prepare a folder to organize the students' work, like a portfolio. Every day, the students produce one, and only one, recording activity. If they did it out of necessity, they put the sheet in the folder, and if not out of necessity the teacher asks them to express what they have learnt on that day, using a list of words, drawings, text, collage, etc., so that the parents may follow their daily progress.

An important aspect is that only one activity of this type is done per day. If the project requires more than one activity on paper, the others will be kept by the teacher, and don't go home. This measure prevents the parents getting accustomed to a great volume of a production on paper and starting to press the staff to produce the same amount all the time, completely taking away the teacher's and the students' pedagogical freedom.

In order to stress the information for the parents and help in understanding the activities carried out at school, which many times are really difficult to understand ("Why is my son checking prices for air tickets to Paris?"), we created a daily class report. At the end of the class, the teacher writes a report regarding the activities of the day and the reasons behind them, which is to be sent to the parents via e-mail. This report has been a big help for the parents to understand the work carried out at school, which generates frequent compliments and contributions, with materials, information and ideas.

EVALUATION

Another key aspect is the evaluation. This is a measuring instrument that is essential for any school concerned with the development of its students. Each class and each student needs to be constantly evaluated, so that small adjustments may be made and some learning opportunities can be chosen over others, in order to correct any deficiency that children may be showing in certain subjects or skills.

The students must participate in the process, perceiving their evolution in solving problems that life presented to them while making their final project, realizing what they have learnt and what they should learn for the new challenges ahead. However, there is a more technical component in the evaluation, which must, for the starting series, be developed by the teacher. I'm talking about the school's goals related to the National Curricular Parameters, implemented in Brazil.

In our school, we've developed software that is installed in a server connected to the internet. Every month the teachers access the system from wherever they are, and insert data on spreadsheets with lists of goals to be reached with their students. For example, one of the goals that part of our students must develop is: "Does the student know the sound of all the letters in the alphabet?". Thus, the teacher indicates which students have already reached this goal. From then on, the system generates reports with a percentage of development of each student and each class, for each of the subjects and skills proposed by the school.

With this system, we impose some our values in the evaluation.

EVALUATION SHOULD BE AN ON-GOING PROCESS

We believe the student should be constantly evaluated by the teacher, so that the evaluation may be more precise and atypical moments in each student's life may not be taken into consideration, thus better reflecting the student's evolution.

As our methodology is very dynamic, we need to look closer at the curves in the process and detect the trends, allowing us faster reactions and more efficiency. The teacher doesn't need to wait for the end of the quarter to assess the result generated by a certain project.

TEACHERS' SELF-EVALUATION

In our opinion, the student must be an active agent in the teaching-learning process, but not responsible for it. The student must be encouraged, guided and supported by the teacher, who must use any need presented by the projects in order to make his students find out the necessary knowledge. This process isn't simple and demands a lot of energy from the teacher, but it's essential to reach the proposed goals. Thus, every month, the teacher evaluates his own work via the students' performance, allowing him to make important corrections to maintain the quality of the learning process.

NO TESTS

Tests should be over. At "Escola do Max," we only have tests (that don't have any value to the evaluation) in order to prepare our students to attend other schools, if they move to another region or city, or so that they can get used to them, as in the future they may have to face college entrance exams ("vestibular") and tests to enter certain careers. However we believe that tests don't represent the student's whole learning process and their assessment is extremely inaccurate, as they capture the student's performance at a certain time, through a very limited volume of information. Even weather conditions, a thunderstorm, may influence the result to be achieved by a student in a test.

Also, life is a lot more than a series of questions and answers. We want our students to understand knowledge as a tool to achieve happiness, something important that must be interiorized, not a lot of information put together to convince someone that we know a certain subject. For that, our students learn interpersonal communication, and are prepared to convince anyone about anything.

PARENTS SHOULDN'T HAVE ACCESS TO THE RESULTS OF THEIR CHILDREN'S EVALUATIONS

To the parents of the students at "Escola do Max," I apologize!

While observing my students and their parents, I have witnessed several situations of great demands and pressure on children, sometimes as young as 3 years old! The parents are anxious and in a hurry, therefore demanding, not only from the school, but from the child, a certain performance which they consider important. For example: parents that had great difficulty in learning English demand from the child greater attention and performance in that subject. Parents that are writers or journalists are extremely demanding regarding the development of the written language. Engineers are demanding with mathematics and sciences, and so on and so forth.

Several times (and I mean several), the parents talk to the child constantly about the subject, demanding greater effort, which frequently generates "extra" activities at home, to no avail, as the child has no problem, except the parents' anxiety.

The children submitted to this situation become insecure, talk less, hide their difficulties and lose their joy in learning. I'm especially concerned with the impacts on self-esteem, because the child thinks: "If my parents don't believe me, why should I believe in myself? They know what they are talking about." This is very sad!

Of course not every child will present such an extreme reaction, but, in order to avoid any level of pressure on the child, I decided that in our school only the pedagogical team has access to the data and, in the case of the elementary school, our students' parents receive report cards with normalized grades.

SELF-ASSESSMENT

However, we'll soon make a change to this system and we'll allow the students to have access to their own evaluation and participate in verifying the results through self-assessment. But we're still discussing how we'll protect children from demanding parents and prepare them to deal with their grades in a more intelligent manner than the one we had when we were students.

Our focus for this change will be on the elementary school, in which children will have access to the system and may manage their goals, looking to, as well as the teacher, make the most of the opportunities brought by the projects in order to comply with their pedagogical goals and acquire knowledge, making their self-assessment with the teacher's support.

In this chapter, we saw the whole step by step process of the work with lifelike projects. In principle, they may seem complex, but in a daily routine they work almost naturally, provided the teacher gives up control and believes in the proposal, leaving children free to create.

The most important point for the teacher to adapt well to this work is that he must have the confidence to develop his activities without having pre-planned them, believing and using the opportunities that will come up from the project's needs in order to make the final project. This work has shown results that are far superior to those obtained with planning and guiding the learning process. After all, human knowledge has a reason to exist. The students in lifelike projects learn things by implementing them at the time when they are necessary or interesting, experiencing the knowledge and learning through life.

SOME CONSIDERATIONS

Maybe the reader finds similarities in our Lifelike Projects methodology with other methodologies based on projects or even methodologies that don't use projects. Several ideas and processes developed by other authors have served as reference to us and even as a base so that we may implement our ideas. Thus, we may consider that our work is like a recycling, in which you search for a different use for the same object. That is to say that we used aspects of different methodologies with an entirely new approach, which would serve the lifelike philosophical purposes.

Among the different references used in our research, we can highlight the work of Judy Harris Helm, Sallee Beneke and their collaborators, in "The Power of Projects" (Teachers College Press), in its Brazilian translation, published by Editora Artmed and entitled "O Poder dos Projetos." We were drawn to the structure used in the projects described, especially the construction of graphics organizing previously acquired knowledge and goals to be reached, as well as the studying sequence, culminating in the final project. We thought it was a very interesting structure, and has greatly influenced the organization of our own methodology, even including the possibility of having the students participating in the decision of certain processes, influencing the choice of themes and activities.

Despite Helm & Beneke's work being aligned with most of our beliefs, we felt that it didn't reach the whole level of freedom we desired, and that it would lead to the experience, and with the teacher's support, to the knowledge and development of skills. As "lifelike supporters," we would like children to be fully in charge of the project, deciding the theme without any interference from the teacher. We didn't like the idea that the teacher could accept or reject the student's idea, according to the teacher's judgment. Also, for us, the project should be an enterprise decided, conducted, completed and evaluated by the students themselves, without the teacher having the power to allow or refusing initiatives according to his own judgment. The so-coveted freedom wasn't a reality.

Another aspect we consider important, and that should be implemented, is having the whole project dedicated to a defined goal established by the children. The sensation of having a goal, overcome obstacles and reach it, would teach the students a lot, developing entrepreneurism, self-esteem, persistency and several other key characteristics for the success of the students in their personal and professional future.

Finally, the theme of the project for us shouldn't be the goal for the project, but the background to achieve a goal defined by the children, and this process of searching becomes the object of study. This would be the only way in which we would be teaching our students to live, so that they could learn to define their own objectives and search for them, using several tools, which are the object of study, such as mathematics, writing/reading skills, entrepreneurism, science, personal communication, emotional intelligence, among so many other things.

Thus, as happened in the Airplane project of one of the classes at "Escola do Max," more than learning how an airplane works, our students decided that they would find ways to see an airplane for real. And, instead of having the teacher organize a field trip to the aero club for the students, our students researched, discussed and managed to find ways to fund, negotiate and organize their trip to the aero club. That is to say, they conquered the power of making things happen. And this is what life is all about.

Therefore, by incorporating elements of other methodologies and redefining their uses, we have created a new methodology. We have developed a specific method to choose the themes for projects. The students follow a sequence of steps that allow them to organize, debate and vote on their ideas for a democratic choice, without the interference of the teacher. Then, they raise their questions and hypotheses, and research in order to obtain a sufficient repertoire to define what they want to reach. This is a completely new use of knowledge in the classroom: to learn in order to decide, to decide in order to make, to make in order to learn, to learn in order to live. In the last phase, the students face the problems and find solutions so that their project may be carried out, celebrating and reaping the fruit.

When the most critical readers perceive elements in our methodology already seen in other approaches, I ask you to look deeper and realize the recycling that has taken place in the procedures and methods, in order to have an entirely new use, aligned with the purposes of the "lifelike" philosophy previously discussed.

Chapter VI

PROJECT
DEEP SEA

The Deep Sea project was carried out by one of the classes at "Escola do Max" together with another class of students of the same age, between 3 and 4 years old. It was an excellent example of how to apply all the concepts of the lifelike approach, with a great development of entrepreneurism and related skills, which allowed the students to go beyond the mandatory contents.

Teacher: Isabela Silva Caputo
Student's age: 3 and 4 years old
Theme: Deep Sea
Objective: Visiting São Paulo Aquarium

The Deep Sea Project was developed at "Escola do Max" in 2009 by the Max II class, comprised of eleven students, in a range of 3-4 years old. The class has 4 girls and 7 boys.

The children chose the theme of the next Project after skimming some magazines.

The reader can see here how the children in this class are ready to face the adverse and frustrating situations, as one of the students, even after having lost in a previous voting session, showed persistency and argued to convince his colleagues to vote for his idea.

It's worth noting that the research related to the theme of the project was very useful to teach science and geography, via which the students could explore several concepts related to sea creatures and their environment.

While choosing the project's theme, the children suggested several themes that interested them, such as motorcycles, dinosaurs, buildings and butterflies, found in several magazines. The "deep sea" theme, however, emerged during the brainstorming session. This theme had been presented at the previous project, but lost out to the "hurricane" theme. The child who had suggested this theme didn't give up and suggested it again to his classmates. While discussing which would be the best theme, this student managed to convince most of the class to choose the "Deep Sea" theme and received 6 votes, while motorcycles had 4, dinosaurs, 2, and butterflies and buildings didn't receive any votes.

We went on, preparing our map with the first questions and hypotheses presented by the children about the deep sea. Over the following days, the students went after the answers. Their questions and curiosities were answered by researching the internet, books, performing experiments, watching documentaries, films and interviews. After the research, the children decided that the final project would be to visit the São Paulo aquarium, where they would be able to see several creatures that they studied in the research step.

After defining the final project, the children had to make it happen! They were all very excited about the idea, but they had no clue of the great journey they had ahead of them in order to reach this goal, after all they would be responsible for all the details of the field trip. Soon, the children realized that they needed information regarding the aquarium: the address, the price of admission, opening hours and the days it was open. The children managed to get this information by calling the aquarium and speaking to the secretary.

At this point, another question came up: how will we get there? Based on this question, we researched the different modes of transport and studied which one would be best. All agreed that the best transport would be a van. Then we needed one! When questioned about who could have a van, the children remembered a colleague that uses this vehicle to go to school. The colleague handed them a card of the person responsible for the transportation and, again, they used the telephone to get in touch with the person responsible for the van and found out how much he would charge to takes us in this field trip. Well, now we already had the total amount we would need in order to go to the aquarium. With the teacher's help, we added the amount of the aquarium's ticket to the amount of the transport per person. Each child would have to pay R$ 30,00. To pay?! When the children faced this problem, they started to argue. Some said they had no money, others said that their parents wouldn't give the money, and others had the idea of selling something. The class liked this solution. Then another discussion started: what would they sell? Jelly? Cake? Then a child mentioned that singers have lots of money. Xuxa, for example, makes a lot of money by selling CDs. Based on that comment, the children decided to record a CD with songs sung by them. "If Xuxa can, why can't we?," they asked me. This question was on my mind. In principle, this sounded crazy, but during the conversation, everything started to become real.

The following day, I heard that my students were making plans to go to the aquarium together with the

The children were constantly encouraged to reflect, from the mode of transport used to how to raise the necessary funds. It wouldn't be a surprise if one of the students suggested using a helicopter to go to the aquarium, and the teacher wouldn't reject this proposition. With that, the children would check the costs of flying in a helicopter, as well as the existence of heliports near the site.

Even the telephone calls were made by the children themselves. Depending on their age, they may have the teacher's help, by introducing the project to the person on the other end of the phone, so that they can understand the school's teaching proposal and answer the students' questions.

class of another teacher, also comprised of 12 children of 3-4 years old, which was developing a project about divers. The other students heard about us going to the aquarium and asked my students if they could come with us. After a meeting between the classes, my students presented our plans to raise money and the other class instantly agreed and asked us the name of the CD. We haven't thought about a name for our CD! Soon two names were suggested by the students: "The Rascals" and "Happy Gang". These two names were put to a vote and the majority chose "The Rascals." With the name of the CD defined, the children celebrated!

The following day, children arrived excited to record the CD, only to realize they didn't have the proper material. Therefore, they prepared a list of materials they would need to record the CD. Then the students went after people who could help them get the materials.

With the materials in their hands, each child chose one song and we started to record. After recording, the students realized they needed to buy blank CDs and also their covers. So, they left the other class responsible for purchasing and funding these materials.

After the materials were purchased, the teacher presented the children the receipt, which was checked. Based on the cost of the materials, the tickets for the aquarium and the transport, we discussed how much we would charge for the CD. Using the golden beads, we presented the total amount each child would need, and soon the children realized they couldn't sell the CD for a price lower than that. We took the opportunity to check the prices of music CDs on the internet

The list of materials was an excellent opportunity for the teacher to work reading and writing skills. The name given to each material had to be written on a sheet by all children, thus allowing them to learn from that opportunity.

A need generated by the project turned out as a great opportunity to teach Math. The students were very motivated to sell their CDs and get the money for the trip. Also, they realized how important it is to make the calculations correctly, in order to establish the CDs' sale price. Therefore, the teacher had everybody's attention to apply her techniques of teaching Math.

and, with all this information, the students reached the price of R$35.00 for each CD.

With the price defined and with the CDs in their hands, the children remembered that they had to prepare a cover. They discussed how this would be done. Seeing other CDs, the children saw that some artists used drawings, photos and text to create the cover. Based on these possibilities, the children voted and most of them decided to put their photos on the cover. Then we requested to borrow the school's camera. Several photos were taken of the children, together and separate. While presenting these photos to the children, most of them decided to use the photos where they were alone. In order to make the cover, the children asked the person responsible for the school's marketing and communication to help them, as he had sufficient knowledge in treating images and graphic design.

With everything ready, it was time to sell. The children were very excited when they went to school, but as the days went by they realized that nobody was buying their CD. During a talk, I raised the question: "But do people know that you're selling the CD?." The children then realized that it was necessary to advertise the product. Based on this need, they created several posters, advertising the CD and put them up throughout the school. They also wrote e-mails and sent to all parents.

The following day, they started to see the result of their marketing campaign. The parents started to order the CD via the children's notebooks and e-mail. The children celebrated each order! The orders were so many that the students started to get confused, they didn't know for sure if they had already ordered

The project is a controlled reflection of life. The students are presented with the same needs that we have in our life, everyday, both professionally and personally. Then they used their creativity, networking, research and entrepreneurism to solve the problems of their enterprises.

that one, or how many CDs they had sold. Then it became necessary to create a list with the names of the people who had ordered the CD. In the end, we counted how many orders had been made. As most of the parents bought more than one CD, more blank CDs were necessary, as well as covers.

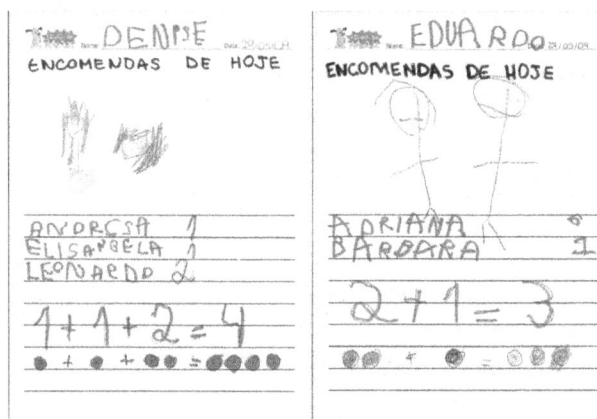

In order to write the list of orders, both literacy and math were studied.

Besides the endless experiences and opportunities to learn the contents that are required by the government, the students develop skills that will be very important in their future, such as persuasion, communication, team work, creativity, amongst so many others, always based on experiencing real situations/problems.

After the orders, it was time to collect the payment. In a meeting, the children had decided to send CDs only after receiving the payment. They decided to send a message to the parents informing them about this decision and, after that, the payment for the CD started to be sent via the children's notebooks. During the payments, the children could see several forms of money, such as notes, coins and checks. They were responsible for checking the money, and registering the payment on the list of orders. During the payment, some parents asked for a discount for buying more than one CD and the two classes had a meeting in order to decide about this issue. Before the meeting, the children asked us what a "discount" was. So, the other teacher and I explained, using experiences the children had had with their parents. After understanding more about the subject, the classes discussed whether they would give the discount or not, and of how much it would be. Having decided everything, the children sent an e-mail to the parents, stating that the discounts would be given for a purchase of more than three CDs.

Having completed the sales, our anxious children agreed to meet with the other class in order to count the money they had collected by selling the CD entitled "The Rascals." And to everybody's surprise, we managed to raise R$ 1,200.00. With that amount we could pay for our field trip to the São Paulo Aquarium, our expenses on materials and we would still have R$350.00!

With the money in their hands, the children called the aquarium to schedule the visit and they were informed that an authorization from their parents was necessary. Right there, they remembered that they are still children and that to go on a field trip, they still needed to ask their parents permission. Based on this need, the children wrote, on a sheet of paper, the authorization request for their parents, informing the place they would visit, the reason for the field trip, date and time for leaving and coming back to school. Over the following days, we were waiting for the authorizations and we celebrated, because everybody sent the authorization back!

After a lot of dedication, effort and anxiety, the day had come! Everything went as planned by the children. The vans were in front of our school at the right time, the staff at the aquarium were wait-

Please note the volume of information that needed to be worked on by the students and the great opportunity of learning was brought by the authorization request.

In my view, this is the greatest advantage of the pedagogical work through lifelike projects: the feeling of pride achieved when the students overcame the challenges and reached their goal. This is the greatest lesson learnt, which is believing in oneself and realizing that dreams are within our reach, and all we need to do is to roll up our sleeves and reach them.

ing for us and the children already had the money, that they earned, to pay for the expenses. At this time, the children didn't hide their feelings of pride and accomplishment. To be honest, neither did I! They managed to solve every obstacle that came up during the whole project, in a creative, mature and entrepreneurial fashion. Now they could enjoy the beauty in the depths of the sea with their friends in the aquarium, seeing all that they have learnt with the research they prepared.

When the children are interested in the theme, they will always be open to new challenges and lessons.

After the field trip, we sat with the children to evaluate our whole project. And when we thought that the project had been completed, the children presented us with an idea to create an exhibition about the "Deep Sea," containing figures of some creatures and texts about their main characteristics, as they had seen in the aquarium. So, the children created a list with the names of the creatures that they would like to present in the exhibition and divided them among the two classes. Each was responsible for five creatures, and my class was responsible for presenting the sea turtle, the stingray, the octopus, the blue whale and the starfish.

In order to make the sea turtle, the children decided to use a collage, with pieces of paper like a mosaic. To create the octopus, they also decided to use a collage, but now with crêpe paper rolled into little balls. They decided to paint the whale and the starfish. For all creatures, they created their "poster" with the information and curiosities that drew their attention.

With all the work of the exhibition ready, the children sent an invitation to their parents, informing them of the day and time of the exhibition. On that day, they chose the best spot in the school to show their work and got ready to receive their guests. The exhibition was such a success that everybody in the school wanted to visit as well. Now our Deep Sea Project was finalized!

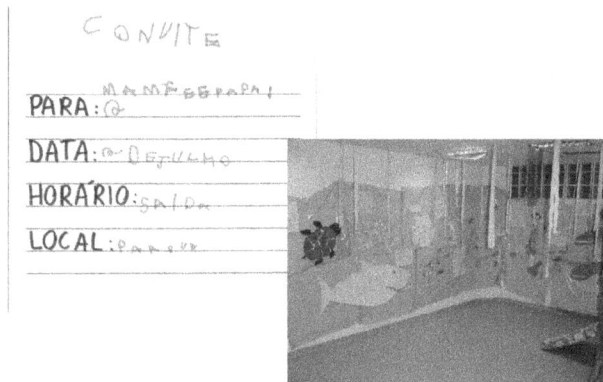

Invitation and exhibition, both were made by the students.

But you may be asking what we did with the money left over from selling "The Rascals" CD. Well, with that money, the children decided to have a picnic at the Botanical Gardens of São Paulo. They negotiated the transport, decided what each student would take, prepared another authorization slip to send to their parents and you know the rest... They couldn't hide their feelings of pride and accomplishment...

Isabela Silva Caputo
Teacher – Pre-school

Chapter VII

PROJECT
CORN PLANTATION

The ideals of the approach via lifelike projects deal with preparing the child for life, and also through life itself, using real situations experienced by the students as a base for teaching. The following project shows how this exposure is feasible under the teacher's supervision, which may allow the student to get in touch with a huge diversity of people, therefore acquiring great cultural baggage that will certainly open many doors in the future.

Teacher: Haryanne Valério
Students' age: 4 and 5 years old
Theme: Corn Plantation
Objective: To plant corn

Another typical day starts. However, for us, the lifelike teachers, something usual wakes us: anxiety. Yes, anxiety, as today we'll be choosing our next project.

It's impossible to foresee what is going to happen. The children start their routine by observing the varied magazines, looking for aspects they already know and looking for things that grab their curiosity. When you least expect it, surprising themes start to emerge. That was how, among so many wonderful projects I have been involved with, the Corn Plantation Project was born.

With it, some amazing questions about corn were presented. Maybe considering the size or weight of an ear of corn is not relevant, in relation to what an adult would be concerned with. Despite this, children between 4 and 5 years old are interested in questions such as these and then we see how important details are for them, besides also realizing how far a child's possibilities can go.

There are so many themes. Among them are the themes of the children's universe, such as toys and cartoon characters. However, during the election of the project's theme, we were immensely satisfied and surprised to see that the "Pokémon" theme lost, by many votes, to the "Corn Plantation" theme. This shows us that we can never underestimate the children's interest in the unknown and the world that is presented before them.

It's interesting to see how much the methodology opens itself to the child. I wonder, would all these questions and the search for answers be possible in other educational approaches?

Sending a fax, an e-mail, a letter or using the school's telephone would be a novelty for any class at the end of the pre-school years. But to communicate with a school thousands of kilometers away, in another country, is even more surprising. Think of the benefits that this fact brings to our students' development.

Regarding the questions that comprised the project's map, I can mention very interesting ones, such as: "Why does corn stand up?", "Does the corn fall off the plant?", or also "Why the little grains are so close together?". But without a doubt, the question that had more repercussions was the following: "How does the seed grow?"

The questions started to be answered via research made by the children during class, using texts taken from the internet and articles found in magazines about agriculture and cattle rearing. The children choose the order of the research, deciding, day after day, which question would be more relevant in a certain moment of time. On the day that the group chose to find out the mystery regarding the seed's growth, we had no idea of what was in store for us.

That day, the children decided to research the internet and, when we wrote the question in the search box, the following option came up: "Students from Godinhaços discover how seeds grows." When we read the article, we found out that those children managed to answer that question by planting peas and beans. The students were interested in talking to the children of the 1st year of an elementary School organized by a church in Godinhaços in order to ask them if the answer would be the same for corn seeds. To our surprise, this school was in Portugal and we found no way to communicate with them via the computer. At this time, the excitement and the anxiety intoxicated the classroom, after all we would be talking to children in another country. Although the children already knew of different modes of communication and were used to using the telephone, writing letters, notes, sending e-mails and faxes, making a telephone call to another country was a novelty.

Before making the call, we looked on an Atlas to find out Portugal's geographical position, which started a discussion about which modes of transport could be used to reach Europe, as one of the students mentioned the possibility of us going there to talk to the students in person. This opportunity also allowed us the opportunity to use the Google Earth tool. Through it, we selected the location of the school we were ready to get in touch with to talk about the seed's growth. Via this tool, we had a view of the Earth and, then, Portugal. Then the city of Godinhaços and, finally, the district of Atães. We then found the school in Godinhaços. By visualizing the territory, all students noticed the differences between our area and theirs, indicating the presence of several trees and plantations in Portugal and several buildings here in São Paulo. We also checked which language we would use to talk to them and the class was surprised to see that we could communicate normally, after all in Portugal they also speak Portuguese.

So, we made the call and we spoke to one of the students at the school. He explained to us that the seed is born from the embryo, which is something alive that needs water to grow, because the water softens the seed coat so that the embryo is able to sprout. For the children, this process brought about more gains from the ones related to contents referring to Science classes; for them, to discover that children living on the other side of the Atlantic can have the same questions as them was impressive, after all, they all found out that we are the same and that we should take the ideas and thoughts of fellow human beings into consideration.

Children, after being motivated by their project, and thinking about the meaning of the activities, open up and put a lot more effort into the learning process. In this case, Geography was the subject involved.

The teacher here indicates a very important aspect. The world is increasingly more globalized, so we should try and develop in our children a better understanding regarding the diversity of cultures and the differences, similarities and opportunities that arise from sharing experiences with other nationalities, preferably through experiencing and living closely to these cultures.

The research through the interviews generated opportunities to develop reading and writing skills, geography and communication skills.

This question was answered, but there were still others to be researched. In order to solve these questions, one of the students had an excellent idea: to visit a corn plantation and talk to the producer in person.

We then had to find out where we could find a corn plantation. In order to find this, the children had to use the field research, where they asked every adult in the school if anyone knew of a corn plantation that we could visit. With that, a list of places was produced by the children, containing the hypotheses described by each one. Everyone gave very similar answers, such as "on a farm," or "in the country side". With these answers, the children were realizing that a corn plantation could be out of reach for the group. But, when we questioned the school's security guard, we had a surprise: there was a corn plantation in an open area in the same street as our school. Yes, a corn plantation in a residential district in the city of São Paulo.

The list of places where corn can be found.

We then started to plan our trip to the other side of the road. With that, we had another great opportunity to work reading and writing skills, as we had to write an authorization slip, to be sent to the parents, asking for permission to cross the street. With this exercise, each student wrote their own note, and then we wrote a common text, through which it would be possible to review the phonetics of each syllable and also work with structuring, cohesion and coherence of a text.

In the corn plantation, the children asked questions to the producer.

Our visit was very productive. The questions were written down by the students and some children, who at the time were already reading, were the speakers of the group, reading the questions directly to the producer. He was a simple person, but with great knowledge, and the told us about some particularities of the corn and how to maintain a plantation.

Soon after the field trip, we could reaffirm a wish

Contrary to the Deep Sea Project, the Corn Plantation project offered opportunities to use mathematical operations outside the financial scope. Each project is unique, with different learning-teaching opportunities, which, however, allow the same concepts to be worked. In this case, mathematical operations.

that came out right at the beginning of the project: to make our own corn plantation inside the school.

The place chosen was the recently built allotment close to the school's block. As no other class had started to plant anything yet, the children proposed to divide and mark the allotment for everyone in school. It was a great opportunity to introduce concepts regarding fractions, as we needed to measure the area and divide it into seven equal parts, representing the amount of teachers responsible for classes at the time. We then needed to divide our own space, as we had learnt at the corn plantation, we should plant the seeds in equal spaces, with four seeds in each hole, therefore generating another great opportunity to work with fractions and multiplication.

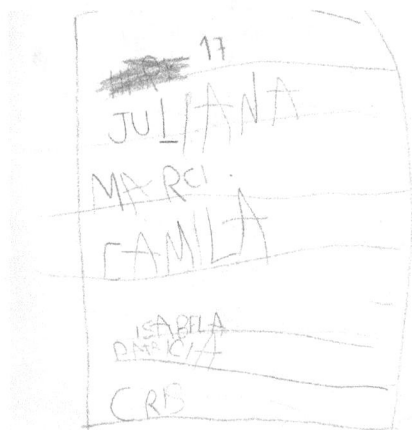

Dividing a sheet of paper in seven parts, each part for a teacher as if it was the vegetable garden, the children have learned the concept of fraction.

The contact with specialists and people working outside the school represent an excellent opportunity for the students to develop communication skills and open their view beyond the school's gates.

After measuring the spaces and making several calculations, we had another question: after all, where would we find corn seeds? The children's main question was that they had never seen a seed store, but with the help of another teacher, we found out that we needed to look for an agronomist.

We found out that agronomists know several techniques to take care of the soil and that they also know a lot about seeds. We managed to get the e-mail address of an agronomist and, thus, the children wrote to him, asking for his help to find a seed store. When the answer arrived, we found out that there were several stores specialized in selling seeds. However, in order to get some corn seeds, it wouldn't be necessary to go to a store. All we had to do was to let an ear of corn dry in the sun.

While the ear was drying, we started to prepare the soil for planting. In order to enrich the soil, we did as the owner of the corn plantation taught us: we separated a lot of fruit skin and added them to the soil. We also mixed the soil very well, so that it would receive air. Besides the manure, we also added some worms to the soil, using this opportunity to learn about the life and the biological role of that creature.

With everything ready and with the dried ear, we started our plantation. We re-measured the distances of each hole and counted the necessary seeds, but now concretely. Each one was responsible for a part of the planting process, making it possible for us to finalize our project by planting corn.

Nowadays, our plantation is growing strong and is watered every week, besides receiving new manure from time to time.

However, it wasn't only corn that was planted in that soil. We also planted faith and hope, as we discovered that we can learn from children in other countries and from humble people with lots of life experience, besides getting information from specialists in that subject. We then learnt that we are all the same and that we can improve the world by helping one other, to be able to see it become strong and beautiful, just like our lovely corn plantation.

Haryanne Valério
School teacher – Pre-School

Chapter VIII

PROJECT FISH

The current view on the potential of children is far superior to that of the previous generations, but it's still appalling to see how much children are underestimated in all areas of life: family, social and, mainly, the educational scope. This project allowed not only the teacher, but also the rest of the school, to stop and rethink and update their view about a child's potential, even at their early age. The understanding of the processes involved in purchasing materials and assembling a fish tank, as well as the great capacity to overcome obstacles and create, which were so joyfully shown by the students, is irrefutable proof of how we can free a child's thoughts and expect surprising and wonderful things. We can really trust our little ones.

Teacher: Juliana Leite
Students' age: 2 and 3 years old
Theme: Fish
Objective: Assembly of a fish tank

For me, this was one of the most important life-like projects of the class. The children voted to study "fish," and something that startled us was the class' unanimity. The students justified their choice by explaining that they consider these creatures to be one of the nicest, which made them more attractive to research and find out more.

Once the theme was defined, we started to work on the project's map. Together we listed several questions and hypotheses, always from the children's perception. The curiosity they had regarding fish was clear by the things they said and in each new question or research they proposed in this stage of the project.

Then, the group was offered different types of materials. Among them all, the most used were technical/specific magazines about fishing and books that dealt with animals and general knowledge.

At the same time, with their parents' help, the children looked for and brought to school several pieces of information regarding characteristics, habits and physical aspect' of the fish, such as habitat, feeding habits, body coverage etc.

The teacher's initiative of bringing a fish to the classroom so that the students could answer their questions by themselves makes the subject not only more concrete, but also a lot more interesting. Usually, with the evolution of the lifelike projects, the children themselves suggest this type of activity. Thus, especially with the younger students, it's key that the teacher expose them to the most diverse possibilities, so that they may start to see beyond what is obvious.

One of the questions on the map that was most intriguing to them was regarding the body of the fish. Children at that age still need and are most interested on concrete aspects, and nothing could solve this question better than having an actual fish in the classroom. And that's what we did: we brought a fish direct from the street market to the school, and, with it within their reach, the children could observe it, touch it and analyze it.

Based on this, they extracted several pieces of information: they felt the fish's texture, they found out that those were scales and they could see that it was different from other animals, which had hair or feathers. Also, the children wanted to know how the fish can breath under water, and they saw that, instead of a nose, fish have gills.

Each day and after each step, the group put in more effort. It was very funny, contagious and gratifying to see them working as a team in the classroom and asking for their relatives' and friends' help in order to have our goals complied with in the best way possible.

One of the high points of this project was the election of the final project: the purchase of a fish tank, so that they could have a real fish, and keep it as the class' mascot.

As this decision was being made, we talked at length and used several other voting processes so that we could democratically decide regarding the final project, such as the color, the breed, the gender and the size of the fish, amongst other aspects.

The class chose a red fish. Thus, one of the preliminary research activities in this phase was to find out which fresh water fish are red. The size would also be an important factor to be observed, as the chosen fish would have to fit in a fish tank of acceptable dimensions for the space available at school. Here we used mathematical concepts in order to calculate the size of a fish tank that would fit the space we had.

A simple trip to the pet shop can be incredibly rich when well used, always respecting the meaning of what is being presented to the students and their motivation and curiosity before, during and after the trip.

In order to answer these questions and to choose the proper fish, the children decided to visit a pet shop. In order to do that, we needed to request the parents' authorization and also money for the transportation. The use of written language was worked with them while creating the note requesting authorization, and oral communication was developed when the students needed to get in touch with the driver who would drive them to the shop.

There, the students talked to the person in charge, who indicated to them which fish they could buy that was red and male, characteristics that they had already voted upon. The students could also list the items they would have to buy and their prices. Thus, we could calculate how much money would be necessary for the purchase. Through this activity, we worked mathematical concepts and language skills, when we listed the name of materials, their prices and calculated the total amount.

In the shop, the children solved their doubts and chose a fish with certain qualities that could be raised in an aquarium in the classroom.

When encouraged, the entrepreneurial spirit comes naturally to children, who search for creative solutions in order to obtain the necessary resources to realize their enterprise. In this case, to sell jelly was an ingenuous solution that one of the students, of this class ageing 2 to 3 years old, wisely found.

When we went back to school, interactions between the students in the classroom were impressive, based essentially on discussions about how to get the necessary amount to buy the fish tank and the mascot.

Regarding this, the students found a solution to their problems through cooking, and as suggested by one of the children in the class, they decided to make jelly to sell.

First of all, we had to make a test to see how many portions we would be able to make with a recipe of jelly, so that we could calculate how many we would have to sell. For that, we used concrete mathematics: by using small materials that represented the prices we discovered on our field trip, we calculated how much jelly we would have to sell for the amount of R$ 1.00.

Then, the children organized the sale. This activity excited the whole class, including the teacher and school employees due to the great satisfaction of seeing the success of our children's enterprise: parents requested more jelly and they had to organize a second day of sales, resulting in double the amount they needed.

This exposure to parents and other employees in the school encourages the children to become more expansive and communicative, as when they are anxious to achieve their goals, they control their shyness and start to become more interactive socially. All these aspects will make a great difference to their future, both professionally and personally speaking.

Before the sale, the students hang advertising posters on the walls.

Due to the higher amount generated, we were able to buy two fish of different colors, instead of only one, a larger fish tank and all the items listed that would be necessary to maintain these fish.

The time arrived to assemble the tank. The dedication and excitement of the students during the preparation and the assembly not only surprised us: it left us all emotional. Particularly speaking, I confess that it was one of the nicest activities, with the most gratifying results I have experienced so far. The sparkle in the children's eyes left no doubt that they were enchanted with the activities.

As a teacher, it was a great pleasure to see the evolution of those children, so small in size, but at the same time, so developed and, at many times, so mature for their age!

Upon realizing the countless benefits presented by the methodology for the development of their children, the parents leave their insecurities and prejudices aside and actively adhere to the children's enterprises, performing a very important role, as stimulating parties, not only for their children, but also for the teacher and the school as a whole.

Even the shiest children evolved a lot in the art of communicating, via the need to use the telephone, letter, e-mail and even fax when we needed to research fish, the prices and necessary materials, besides asking for their parents and the principal office's authorization

Here I need to highlight the invaluable cooperation from all parents. Their intense participation, with concrete actions, and mainly by the support they gave their children, was very important for the excellent result we achieved.

Through this project, we were able to try, in a very clear manner, the ideals of the lifelike ideology: to not think only in the immediate formation and development of purely academic activities, but to also to work towards impacting, directly or indirectly, the preparation of these children for a more sustained action in the future.

Important values could be seen in these activities, such as the class' self-knowledge while a team, and of each student as a member of a team, developing a strong sense of collaboration and team work which will be key for their professional future.

Objectively speaking, the class experienced important additional knowledge, among them the reflection regarding the different styles of communication, after all they had very clear objectives to reach, either in the sale of their jelly or while researching prices and materials. They also developed the exercise and the understanding of different forms of leadership and responsibilities of taking decisions as a group, learning to respect the diversity of opinions and differences. The children showed great maturity, when they managed to decide together issues such as choosing which fish to buy.

Personally, I was very satisfied with the objectives that the class reached with this project, the aspect of school formation and also under the point of view of developing personal and interpersonal skills, the improvement in the dynamic of the group/class and the creative and innovative intervention of each one of the students.

Juliana Leite
Teacher – Pre-School

Chapter IX

PROJECT UNITED STATES

The methodology through lifelike projects allows a different learning process and is very entertaining at different levels and applications, including learning languages. In this project we realized how rich it can be to teach English via this methodology.

Also, the Project United States taught us an important lesson about dealing with the children's frustration in their enterprises, especially when they choose final projects that are impossible or not feasible to be carried out at that time.

Teacher: Manuela Neves
Students' age: 4 and 5 years old
Theme: United States
Objective: Visit Disneyworld

This project was conducted in the English classes of a class of children of 4 and 5 years old. Therefore, it was developed in English, having The United States as the theme, which was chosen by the class through the presentation of images in magazines. The students chose this theme because they saw a photo of the flag of the United States and they recognized it, as they already knew something about that flag: they knew which country it represented, and that the language they were learning, English, was the language spoken there.

When they chose this theme, the children showed their interest in what they were learning - English - and the fantasy world they knew from there: Disneyworld. They presented this idea while they were building the map with the questions regarding that country. Also, they showed a lot of interest regarding the modes of transport that would allow a trip

The reader should pay special attention to the fact that, in this case, as the classes were in English, the teacher was mostly interested in opportunities to teach English and the cultural characteristics involved.

between Brazil and the United States. Those were the three main points raised by the students when they were creating the map.

Before answering the questions prepared by the children, we started our research by analyzing the flag of the United States, after all that was the reason why they chose the theme. With this analysis and a map of the United States, the children wanted to see the Brazilian flag and map. Using a map of the Americas, we saw that the two countries were very far from each other and that it wouldn't be simple to get there. Each student made their own reproduction of the US flag.

Using a map, the children could observe the distance between Brazil and The United States.

Then we started to answer the children's questions about the modes of transport which would allow a trip from Brazil to the USA. We started by suggesting a car and we found out that it is indeed possible to go by car: all you need to do is cross a bridge over the

Panama canal or take a ferry. The children were really curious at this point and, once again, we went back to the map to see if there really was no way to get there without crossing water. However, as we found out, this crossing takes a long time. To go by boat, all you need to do is follow the coast. The helicopter would need to land in several places, as it can't fly long distances. Finally, the airplane seemed to be the most appropriate mode of transport and some children were able to confirm from personal experience: they had been to the United States by airplane.

It was very interesting to realize the huge vocabulary that the project opened up for us, not to mention the Geography lesson that, though it wasn't one of the teacher's objectives, was presented in English.

All this talk was in English. Knowing the vocabulary regarding the modes of transport, the children could focus their learning on forming sentences: without realizing, while they listen to the teacher, they are learning the internal grammar of the language, i.e., how sentences are structured. In order to learn what they wanted, they needed to understand what we were reading and talking about in English.

After we answered every question prepared by the children, one of them brought to the class texts in English and photos from Disneyworld. We read the texts out loud about its history, we interpreted the texts and we saw the photos. With this, the children had the opportunity to once again, see not only the vocabulary, but the sentences as a whole and their structure. They already knew the characters, so what was being said about them? They needed to understand English as a whole, and not only the words.

Although the material wasn't necessary for the project, the children were curious about the issue. As the teacher had the students' interest and motivation, and their curiosity was linked to the project, she decided to develop the information.

The fact that the children were curious about the modes of transport and Disneyworld made it clear, from the start that their interest in the project was to go to the USA. That's what they decided when the time came to choose their final project: they would

This is a very significant case of the careful work that the teacher should have when dealing with impossible final projects. At the time, the children were putting all their hopes on a trip we knew would be impossible.
As described in a previous chapter, this type of situation, which can cause frustration must be conducted by the teacher in order to prepare the children for the frustrations of life, without losing their capacity of persistence, but on the contrary, to accept impossible things that life presents us . After all, frustration is part of life.

take a trip to Disneyworld.

We, the adults, knew that that idea wouldn't be feasible, but the children had the opportunity to find out for themselves whether they could go or not and, most importantly, why.

While some wanted to get immediately on the airplane, others knew that it wouldn't be possible. We had to pack, have money, choose the date, book rooms in hotels, buy the tickets, request parents' authorization, etc.

In each of these preparation stages, their knowledge of English was developed based on their interest in the trip. When we decided what we would take in the bags, we learnt vocabulary regarding clothes. We saw the calendar to be able to schedule the date for the trip, therefore reviewing the numbers in English and learning the days of the week. We looked on the internet for the prices of tickets, hotels, food, and extra things that they decided.

It was during this stage that the children started to realize that their final project would not be feasible. Since taking the decision to travel to the United States, some students came to school stating: "My father told me that I won't be able to go." Many students couldn't explain why and, therefore, the others carried out the plans.

When we calculated how much the trip would cost, the children were surprised. Even without having the exact concept of that number, they realized that the number written in the black board was huge, so it should be a large sum of money. In order to clarify this point, they asked some teachers if the amount of money was really that large, which was confirmed to them: they started to say that they didn't have that much money.

Some students said that they had lots of coins in their piggy banks and that they could pay for the trip. We discussed if those coins would be enough to pay for so many costs and they realized that they wouldn't. Other students suggested that they could sell something in order to get the money.

We used the mathematical concepts to calculate how much they earned from their sales in other projects, and we realized that the amount was a lot less. Then they decided to ask another class for some ideas, but all calculations resulted in amounts that were far below what they needed. Finally, they decided that their parents could pay for the trip, and they all agreed.

Then we decided to write a letter to the parents asking money for the trip. Also, we would ask for their authorization, allowing their children to take the trip. We didn't get into details over legal aspects, but the children knew that they needed written authorization from their parents to be able to travel abroad without them.

When we were writing the letter, we began to teach the class how to write in English. The names of the letters were introduced, as well as the sound of some of them, we wrote the words on the black board and they tried to read while they were copying the note to their parents.

The letters returned with several negative answers. The parents stated that they didn't have enough money or that they didn't want their children to travel by themselves. For those who didn't have enough money, the students soon had a solution: those that had money would pay for those who didn't.

At this time, it's important to highlight two interesting facts. The first is the volume of information the students are acquiring while planning this trip, and the clear motivation around everything they develop. Several opportunities to teach math, English, communication, science and geography are arising at this time.

The second aspect deals with frustration. The readers must note that the teacher is letting them learn the facts little by little, and that they are realizing by themselves that the enterprise would not be feasible. They are not hearing a "no" from an adult, they are realizing through the facts that they will not be able to travel. As everything is being done one step at a time, and respecting the maturity and perception of each child, the frustration is under control and it brings important lessons.

Using multiplication, we calculated the total amount of the trip: there were thirteen students in the class, and each would need an X amount of money for the trip. That is to say that thirteen times the amount for each child would be the total price of the trip. If the previous number had already been a surprise, when they saw that new value, they knew that they wouldn't be able to pay.

When they realized the trip was impossible, frustration crept in. To a certain degree, they were already prepared for the inevitable answer: they knew a lot of money was necessary, they knew how difficult it was to travel to such a distant destination without their parents, and they started to wonder whether they would be going. For these reasons, only a few transformed this frustration into anger and showed sadness. But soon after, when they saw their classmates accepting the situation, these children started to deal with the feeling in a better way.

The teacher dealt with this frustration in the proper way, in order to renew the children's entrepreneurial and persistent spirit.

We then discussed together about this question of us not being able to travel to Disneyworld. Would this be a permanent "no"? Could the plans be only postponed, instead of cancelled? They reached the conclusion that they could save money and, one day, take this trip with their parents or wait until they grow older and go by themselves. After this discussion, the children were excited again and learnt an important lesson: the fact that they can't go now doesn't mean that they had to give up. It was an essential work to develop persistency in the children.

At this point, the children showed their maturity and understood the situation. We reached the "no" via a process, and they had already been prepared for that. They had the maturity to start realizing that it would be difficult to go on this trip. Had the "no" been presented immediately after the idea and the children wouldn't have understood and they would have been a lot more frustrated.

In order to try to not end our project like this, on a frustrating note, the children started to have several ideas. One suggested we drew the Disney characters, another wanted to build a castle, but the final idea came from one of the children that had not accepted the "no" at first: we could make puppets representing the characters and a castle-shaped scenario. Everyone loved that idea.

The children drew the castles they were going to build.

At first, the children chose their characters; each one of them already had their favorite one and didn't even seem to remember the trip. They suggested that we created the puppets with old socks, which they would bring from home.

Then with the socks, we reviewed the vocabulary referring to the parts of the body that each puppet would have. We also reviewed the clothing vocabulary before creating the clothes that the puppets would be wearing. We also worked, during the whole time, the names in English of the materials that were being used and the pieces created.

In order to build the castle, the children decided to use small boxes and create the towers, the bridges, flags, everything we had seen in photos and that they already knew how to say in English. They decided to use juice boxes that most of them took for snack time. However, the class alone couldn't bring in enough boxes for the whole castle.

Once again we used mathematical concepts to count how many boxes would be necessary for each child, and then we found out the total for the class. It was too many boxes for them, and for that reason they decided to ask other classes to help them. In English, they went to the other classes to ask their friends to save the boxes for them.

At the end of the production, they were extremely excited about the puppets and their castle, which made it very clear that the whole frustration about not travelling to Disneyworld had been overcome. Nobody took this idea out of their heads: they realized it by themselves that it would be impossible, and then, they managed to have another idea to finalize the project, without frustration preventing them from having fun. And that was exactly what they had in the end: lots of fun!

Manuela Neves
English Teacher

Chapter X

ENTREPRENEURISM, NEEDS AND OPPORTUNITIES

HOW ARE THE PEDAGOGICAL OBJECTIVES
REACHED IN THE PROJECTS?

"To be an entrepreneur is a lot more than just having the will to reach to the top of a mountain; it is understanding the mountain and the size of the challenge; planning each detail of the climb, knowing what you need to take with you and which tools to use; finding the best trail, being committed to the result, being persistent, calculating the risks, getting physically prepared; believing in your capacity and starting to climb."
Learn how to learn. Entrepreneurial Brazil Program

This mountain can be a pharmacy, a bakery, a newspaper, an industry or even a traineeship in an important company, conquer a loved one, raise money for a trip, beat a disease, fund resources for an important social cause, among other infinite possibilities in which "being entrepreneurial" may represent the difference between success and failure.

Several people, especially those that manage companies, see as "entrepreneurial" only those people who carry out their own enterprises or businesses within larger companies. I, on the other hand, prefer to consider "entrepreneurial" people who make things happen, who overcome difficulties to build the necessary scenario to achieve their goals, creating opportunities, raising funds, articulating resources and overcoming obstacles.

My justification for that is the observation of how people with an "entrepreneurial spirit" deal with other types of problems and projects outside the business scope. These people face difficulties and challenges from another point of view and approach that, in my opinion, is due to their "entrepreneurial spirit," which allows them to usually perform better than the rest in these issues.

In most articles and books about entrepreneurism we find a broad approach on the difficulties faced by the entrepreneurs and their challenging stories, usually connected to lack of capital, information, relationship, etc. A lot is talked about "entrepreneurial profile" and its inherent characteristics, even showing the possibility of developing these characteristics in people that were not born with them.

While I consider the contemporary view of entrepreneurism and the possibility of developing it in the "common man" to be excellent, I believe that the whole literature available is very shallow in dealing with the psychological issues involved with the entrepreneurial profile. In my opinion, it's necessary to have a deeper analysis of the aspects that make an entrepreneur.

Of course my motivation for this approach is, clearly, the development of the entrepreneurial profile in children, especially in the final years of pre-school and during elementary school. However, in order to do that, I consider my broader definition of the "entrepreneurial profile" and its implications not only in a professional capacity, but especially in one's personal life, as the latter is the starting point for any professional project. I would like to remind that, in the lifelike ideology, we deal with life as a whole and making personal dreams come true, searching for happiness in any scope of the life of a human being.

The literature available lists the main aspects of the entrepreneurial profile such as, among others:

Self-confidence
Initiative
Risk Taking
Self-motivation
Vision
Team work
Dedication
Curiosity
Organization
Leadership
Creativity

Flexibility
Persistency
Autonomy
Optimism
Capacity of analysis

After listing above the aspects which define the entrepreneurial profile, I invite the reader to reflect. Would people that have the characteristics listed above have the same way of facing their problems and difficulties, whatever the scope is, personal, professional or family related, as other people?

Therefore, I'd rather have a more comprehensive view of entrepreneurs, considering the benefits of their characteristics to their whole life. Therefore, I deal with entrepreneurism as a profile we want to develop in our students, included in the pedagogical objectives of our lifelike ideology and methodology. Thus, children in the future will be able to open their own business, or not, and it will be their decision. However, they will have the necessary skills to do whatever they like in whatever scope they wish, be it professional or personal. And this will be a powerful tool in building their happiness.

ENTREPRENEURISM AS METHOD AND SUBJECT

Within our lifelike proposal, the entrepreneurism is simultaneously subject and method. We have developed a sequence of objectives directed especially at the development and evaluation of entrepreneurism in the students. However, this theme becomes very important to our methodology via Lifelike Projects, as it is our working method.

As the projects are triggered by subjects that the children are interested in and are totally developed based around a final project, chosen by the children, this project is fully planned, developed and completed by them, with the teacher's supervision.

Thus, our approach via the Lifelike Projects produces an important effect, which is the development of entrepreneurial characteristics and skills. However, as the projects become real enterprises developed by the children, an important door is opened for the contents, whether they are required or not by the Ministry of Education (MEC), and become part of the lesson. After all, we are talking about education, and all the endless knowledge and skills that must be internalized by the students.

NEEDS OR OPPORTUNITIES

All human knowledge comes from a necessity, whether to solve problems or in understanding the world to obtain better opportunities. There is no knowledge without meaning - any serious work of scientific research serves a purpose.

Similarly, we use this knowledge to perform our daily tasks and solve problems, whether that is writing a letter, calculating the domestic budget, negotiating with a supplier, planning a trip, understanding news, etc.

Any pedagogical objective is nothing more than the collection of the knowledge that the students must learn to perform the same roles that us, adults, perform on a daily basis, in the most diverse professions or life styles.

The lifelike projects are nothing more than a reflection of real life, monitored by the teacher. When the children choose a certain final project, they will have to solve the same endless problems and perform a series of roles that us, adults, perform in our day to day lives. This may be writing a letter to the parents trying to convince them to allow the children to go on a field trip they're looking forward to, calculating the budget to building a model Tyrannosaurus Rex, imagining ways to get money in order to finance their enterprise,

projecting sales of pies or lemonade, etc. For each problem generated by their projects, a series of knowledge and skills will be necessary, such as Written Language, Mathematics, Geography, Science,
Communication, amongst others. All the objectives defined in MEC's
National Curriculum are included, plus others which should also be
required, so that the children may have an education to match the
contemporary world.

Thus, each necessity of the project is, in fact, a learning opportunity that must be embraced by the student, so that the learning
process can start. Please note that I didn't say here that the "teaching-learning" process, because in our approach the students learn by
themselves, with the teacher's support. Of course, we must respect
the limits of the children of each age group.

Therefore, in our methodology, the pedagogical objectives are
reached in the following sequence:

Entrepreneurism ⇒Needs/Opportunities⇒ Study ⇒ Learning

In most approaches to learning through projects, the sequence
of development is the same. However, as the students don't participate in the decision-making process of any stage of the project, thus
having a totally passive role, entrepreneurism is not developed, and
neither are any of its valuable characteristics. Also, if there is no full
motivation and meaning, the method's efficiency is reduced in comparison to the potential available.

In the other methodologies, which represent the majority of the
learning techniques adopted by schools, the situation is even worse
and the process can be summarized as:

Teaching⇒ Learning

And this puts the student as a mere passive absorber of human knowledge. Also, content not required by the government is not

developed, further impoverishing the education.

Therefore, I suggest the approach via lifelike projects as a way to expand the educational reach, in order to:

> Increase the amount of themes covered
> Include contemporary themes and skills
> Prepare the students for the real world
> Capture the students' interest and get them involved
> Develop entrepreneurism
> Develop their self-esteem
> Develop initiative
> Guide the students to success
> Build a new society

SPECIFIC SUBJECTS

The most attentive reader will ask: "What should we do when a specific and important subject needs to be taught, but it doesn't arise in the project?"

When we were developing our methodology, this was a very frequent concern. However, for preschoolers and those in the first years of elementary school, which is the current public of "Escola do Max," there haven't been any classes that have finished the year without having covered almost all themes in the curriculum – at least once.

Therefore, in very few cases the teacher had to intervene in the sense of having to direct some project in order to develop an activity that didn't represent a genuine need for the project. Though infrequently, these situations do happen, and our conduct is to talk to students and let them know about our "maneuvering" and its necessity, and because these situations are really rare, the students readily understand the problem and allow parallel activities to be developed, or even projects with predefined themes. In that last case, with a final project defined by them.

However, for the series before the 5th year of elementary school, we can count on one hand the number of times when we had to use this resource.

We're currently studying how to apply the methodology to the later series of the elementary school or even for high school. We soon expect to be able to share with the reader the knowledge generated by this research and development. However, we can suppose that our conclusions will be around the same values that define our life-like ideology, in which education must be done for life, and through life, always taking into consideration the students' right to choose and actively participate, allowing that there is motivation and meaning in everything that is carried out inside or outside the classroom.

POST-SECONDARY SCHOOL

We see a specially promising future for our methodology in post-secondary schools. Although it's necessary for universities to fully review their teaching models, we can imagine longer lasting projects, in which the students will have to look for the necessary basic knowledge to carry out the projects they chose within the area of their course, as seen currently in the graduate courses.

Therefore, each challenge that the students will have to face to pursue their projects will bring endless needs and learning opportunities, which may be guided, though not conducted by the teacher.

Even the development of skills will be a lot more intense, which includes the entrepreneurial profile, as there will be a greater need for the students to pursue knowledge by themselves. As a consequence, we would have more independent and secure professionals, with a lot more initiative, adding a lot more value to the institutions to which they may belong in the future.

Chapter XI

THE LIFELIKE TEACHER

In order to show the transformation which the teacher under goes when he starts to work with a lifelike proposal, I'll include a testimonial from one of our newly-hired teachers, Tatiana Rodrigues, who, when this book was being written, was experiencing, for the first time, this new methodology of teaching.

"I have recently started to work with Lifelike Projects. I've always considered myself to be an educator open to new ideas, democratic, creative, taking the view that children need opportunities in order to make choices, so that they can face life in the future. To be capable of making decisions, choosing the best ways, respecting the individuality of those around us are all goals that I try to reach, based on a work to build such attitudes that I find to be very important for the world in which we live.

When I started working with the Lifelike proposal, I realized that I could reach greater heights. I saw that the children had the possibility of being more independent than I could ever have imagined before... I was anxious in the beginning, I won't deny it, as open and democratic as I may be, to enter a classroom without anything planned, without presenting ideas that I consider to be interesting for my students, was something very intriguing to me...

In this type of work, I was able to see that the children were the "planners" and that they didn't need me to help them organize themselves and choose themes in which they were interested, in order to be studied.

It's very interesting to realize that my role in the classroom was that of a simple adult that had the capacity to supply the necessary tools for the children so that they could carry out the projects they have created and organized... My role there, at that time, was to make the most of the situations that were arising and thus develop and execute content required by law. My senses had to become really sharp so that I didn't miss any opportunity that arose during each project.

*As an educator, I can say that observing children becoming entre-
preneurs, facing problems like those presented to adults in a very
pleasing and realistic manner, is just lovely."*

Tatiana Rodrigues
Teacher – Elementary School

I chose this testimonial because, through it, the teacher clearly
points out the new role acquired and its impact on her.

ANXIETY AND INEXISTENCE OF LESSON PLANS

In the lifelike proposal, we broke a very rigid rule, powerfully
rooted in all institutions that form teachers: there is no education without lesson plans. Until now, teachers wouldn't even enter a classroom
without having previously established what they were to develop, the
concepts they would intend to pass on to the students, the activities to be executed and the goal they wanted to achieve. However,
we broke this rule by transferring all these decisions to the children,
who explore the world motivated by their curiosity and dreams, without taking into consideration what must be complied with in terms of
an educational program. It's up to the teacher, then, to embark on
this trip and make the most of the situations that arise to teach and
comply with the educational goals required by the school and the
Government.

At this point, the reader needs to be aware of the magnitude of
this change and the insecurity it brings. The teacher must simply enter a classroom with a vague idea of what he will do, supported only
by a final project that the students intend to carry out. However, the
teacher must have in mind that the paths covered to reach this final
project may change at any time, with any student having a new idea
and the rest of the class supporting him, so that they can achieve

what they want to, in a faster or better way.

This situation generates great anxiety and insecurity. "What am I going to do with them today?"; "Will I be able to achieve the goals?"; "How will I make them learn?"; are the questions that haunt the teacher who is adapting to teach via lifelike projects.

However, the teacher needs to relax and enjoy the process. In this approach, the teacher teaches through life, through situations that result from the problems that the students themselves face to carry out their enterprises. It's a process more similar to the education offered by parents, in which daily life raises questions and needs, which are used by them to teach.

In order for teachers to be able to easily adapt to this new proposal, they should trust in life. They should realize that knowledge, especially the knowledge required for preschoolers and pupils in the first years of elementary school, comes from basic needs and, thus, is present in most of the obstacles that come up in the path proposed by the child. The teachers should, then, have clearly and readily available all the objectives that must be reached so that, at the right time, they can develop them with the children, who will realize the need to learn the concept in order to overcome the obstacle that is in front of them.

MOTIVATION

"In the Lifelike approach, we can free ourselves from ABC books and routines, which is exactly what the educators long for. Nowadays we can offer the best things for our students, who don't only play and learn how to read and write, but also learn more about life."

Manuela Neves
English Teacher

At the same time as causing anxiety, the lifelike approach leaves teachers highly motivated and satisfied, as they realize that they can go a lot further, that one day won't be the same as another, that education can be a lot more than that which is proposed in universities.

The lifelike teachers work in an environment which is a lot more fun, they savor every moment with greater enthusiasm, with the same meaning as their students, because they see themselves as part of something greater, as besides learning math, for example, their students learn how to calculate a budget for a project which they themselves created, which makes them apt to join knowledge to personal achievement, i.e., to use the learning process as a way to attain their objectives.

There is no educator by vocation who wouldn't be enchanted by such an achievement and, this is the reason why the pleasure to teach becomes a passion for life, exploring the world and achieving happiness.

KNOWING ONESELF

But the discoveries and the feelings don't stop there. The more I work within the ideas and proposals that we call "lifelike," the more I realize how much the teachers learn. Well, so far that's nothing new, after all every teacher learns (a lot) with their students everyday. However, the lessons learnt by a lifelike teacher are very different.

The lack of routine, the constant changes in the direction of the projects' development process, the uncommon subjects and ambitious ideas dreamt up by the children and the complete absence of lesson plans end up by knocking down all teachers' defenses and rituals, making them look within themselves. The teachers, in order to perform their role well within our proposal, need to concentrate on only one key task: be themselves. And, from there on, live.

This issue may seem banal, but it's amazing how difficult it is for people to be themselves, let go of control and embark on a trip with their students. Initially, most are very insecure, distrustful and afraid. Not having a plan and control exposes the teachers to themselves, and then they find out several aspects of their own personality that they never had realized before.

The great variety of situations brought by the projects is nothing less than the reflection of life and the world. One day they are accounting and celebrating the results of the sale of jelly, the next they are planning a trip to the South Pole. One day they are discussing the characteristics of the corn plantation and the next they are studying principles of aerodynamics in order to build a model airplane. This crazy and random experience transports teachers from one subject to another, enriching their lives. Teachers get out of their home-work routine and become an adventurer exploring the most remote corners of the world, of life and knowledge.

Therefore, dear reader, I may say that the teachers learn, but far beyond the endless concepts they never thought they would study, they learn about life and about themselves, discovering weaknesses, strengths, talents, skills, preferences, and endless aspects about themselves that they have never even imagined they had inside them. And this self-knowledge also becomes an important tool in achieving happiness, inside and outside the school.

CLASSROOM DISCIPLINE

A myth about the lifelike approach is that you can't deny anything to the children, that there is no discipline and that everyone does exactly as they please, whenever they want.

This is not true. In order to achieve things in life, one needs to have a lot of determination, persistency, organization and discipline. Exactly what our ideology tries to teach our students. Therefore, allowing them to disrespect the rules of the school and those of their class, will not help them to reach a solid learning base, achieving all their dreams in the future.

In the lifelike proposal, the students make their decisions, prepare their plans and execute them, but with respect and harmony, in order for them to respect the teachers, their classmates and the social rules of the school and of a healthy relationship. After all, without order it would be impossible to carry out the various activities necessary to reach the final project, which they chose.

Thus, as life is the parameter of our whole ideology, it is present also in our daily routine, in order for the students to learn how to behave properly in each situation, as they will in the future, during a job interview, a business meeting, at an important family dinner, among so many other occasions that will be a part of their personal and professional lives.

TECHNIQUES TO TEACH MATHEMATICS AND READING & WRITING

The reader may have noticed the absence of any comment or even method regarding how the knowledge necessary to the project is passed on to the students.

In fact, taking into consideration especially teaching of mathematics and the reading & writing process, the lifelike proposal doesn't require a specific technique. In this sense, the teachers can use the tools they consider as the most adequate for each class, each child, or even those accepted by the school and the pedagogical coordination. The lifelike proposal intends to bring meaning and motivation to the students, bringing the contents to the surface when they are necessary for the project. However, the technique used by the teachers can be the one they think is the most adequate within the social, educational and pedagogical context.

Within the lifelike proposal, the main techniques derived from the constructivism or other lines, are very adequate. The exception, however, are the techniques derived from more traditional lines of teaching. It wouldn't be possible to develop a list of materials with the students if the school adopts the traditional reading & writing process, in which the letters are presented in the order of the alphabet. However, any methodology could be used if derived from the constructivism or even the phonics method.

The same is valid for mathematics. The teacher must be attentive to see if the concept to be passed on is a necessity of the project, but the technique used to teach it is down to the teacher's discretion.

Thus, the teacher, within certain limits, has great freedom in choosing the best teaching technique, being limited only by content, which should follow the development of the project. This is another advantage of this approach for the teacher.

PERFORMANCE

In general, I have noticed that the teachers are more highly motivated in the approach via the lifelike projects. Even in interviews and dynamics to hire teachers, I notice great curiosity and enthusiasm regarding our methodology, which has been attractive for several professionals that end up being part of our pedagogical staff.

This enthusiasm on the part of the teachers, together with the motivation and the meaning that the methodology has for the student, creates a very positive environment for everyone to get involved, thus having a far superior performance. The results are clearly faster, better and longer lasting, with students and teachers being more satisfied and happier.

Chapter XII

FINAL
CONSIDERATIONS

In this final chapter, after having finished presenting my ideas called "lifelike" and the still short, but not less important, experience in teaching through this ideology, I express my anxiety.

But this anxiety that takes my whole being has nothing to do with whether this book will be a success as a product in the publishing market. Honestly, what I want to do is to be in touch with my students and teachers, to question education, making it evolve. Thus, I'm not really concerned about any financial result that my book may bring me. My anxiety is related to the ideas presented here and their acceptance by the teachers, pedagogical coordinators and school principals, as these are the people who decide on the bases of education and, consequently, the whole future of mankind.

It may be a cliché, but it's also a fact. Through education we can change the world in one or two decades, if only those people who work in the educational area decide to take the right path and have the courage to walk it. However, this is not what we see in most schools. Neglect, economic interests, disrespect for the children and teenagers and short sightedness have been restraining the educational system and preventing any innovation that goes beyond a digital and smart whiteboard. All technology is welcome in the classroom, but it will mean nothing if we don't completely change the way we educate our children. School is outdated, it is (or maybe always has been) very boring! The students don't want to learn and, in several cases, the teachers don't want to teach anymore. We need to recapture the passion for education and realize that the school, the principal's office, the coordination and the teachers need to learn even more than the students. We are stuck in old and useless concepts.

Therefore, my anxiety is for this situation to change. Obviously I don't believe that this book has a solution for education, but, without being modest, I believe that I'm pointing the way in order for this area to evolve. A school should be able to motivate everyone involved in it, becoming an environment for personal and professional evolution. A place in which one can learn beyond the mandatory contents, where it is possible to acquire all necessary tools to reach happiness and build a better world for all of us.

This book may not sell more than a few dozen copies, but I hope this will be enough to plant a seed in people's minds and start a movement causing a revolution within schools, in order to prepare students that love the learning process and personal evolution, students who are prepared to build everything they ever dreamt of, making the world a place for dreams and achievements, with happiness being in first place.

GET IN TOUCH:

LEARN MORE ABOUT LIFELIKE PEDAGOGY
SEND US YOUR DOUBTS AND SUGGESTIONS
PARTICIPATE IN OUR DISCUSSIONS

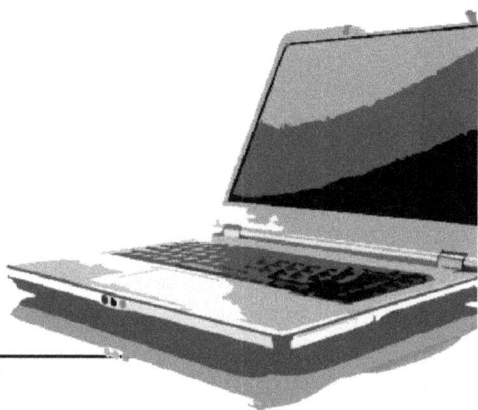

WWW.LIFELIKEPEDAGOGY.COM

ABOUT THE AUTHOR

Marcelo Rodrigues was a curious and alert boy. He walked and talked before his first year and soon showed a great will to explore the environments, opening the doors of the lowest cupboards, what demanded a great attention and energy from his parents.

Still young, he administrated his own lab at the back of his yard, where he produced great amount of colorful liquids, carefully stored in shampoo pots. At this same stage of his childhood, he developed a study about ants, building by himself an anthill in an empty aquarium, where he would feed the ants with quite overstatement while he observed the development of the tunnels and rooms built by these small and interesting animals.

Together with his best friend, he took away the calmness of the neighborhood by exploring, uninvited, the roofs, gardens and yards of the nearby houses, discovering interesting things about his neighbors' lives.

And that's how Marcelo grew up, always curious about what surrounded him, no matter if it was the habits of his neighbors or the ants in the yard.

His constant attempt to understand the world since his childhood became the basis for his great ideas and conclusions about life that persisted until his adult life.

Bibliography

At this point, I would like to thank the reader not only for reading this book, but also for being part of the reflections proposed. I don't expect to influence your thoughts and actions, however I would like the ideas I presented here to trigger new reflections that include breathing life into education, inside and outside the classroom, so that students can experience more and be educated through life. Education is continuously being transformed, and there should always be space for new ways of educating, so that it can evolve at the same speed as the world and society.

The list of references below doesn't translate the whole bibliography I used, but it's a good summary of the main authors who influenced, or that in some way helped the reflections presented here. Although most of the authors are specialists in education, other thinkers, especially philosophers, also had a great impact. A theme that has always generated great interest and obviously was present throughout the whole book is life as an object of study. The relationship between performance and happiness, between social models and the quality of life, has always been a great concern to me, so I've always desired an education dedicated to the quality of life, but with respect to the personal and professional performance and to the social context surrounding us. Therefore, the present bibliography, especially highlighting the philosophers, was of great value to allow me to jump into the adventure of imagining an education based on and directed to a happy life.

ALVES, Rubem. A escola com que sempre sonhei sem imaginar que pudesse existir. 6th ed. Campinas: Papirus, 2001.

ANTUNES, Celso. Nova maneiras de ensinar, novas formas de aprender. Porto Alegre: Artmed, 2002.

ARANHA, Maria Lúcia de Arruda. História da Educação e da Pedagogia: geral e Brasil. 3rd ed. São Paulo: Moderna, 2006.

ARRIBAS, Teresa Lleixà et. al. Translated by Fátima Murad. Educação infantil: desenvolvimento, currículo e organização escolar. 5th ed. Porto Alegre: Artmed, 2004.

BEE, Helen. The Developing Child. Pearson Education. [Translated by Maria Adriana Veríssimo Veronese. A criança em desenvolvimento. 9th ed. Porto Alegre: Artmed, 2003.]

CHEN, Jie-Qi (org.) et. al. Early Learning Activities [Translated by Maria Adriana Veríssimo Varonese. Atividades iniciais de aprendizagem. Porto Alegre: Artmed, 2001.]

CHEN, Jie-Qi (org.) et. al. Building on Children's Strengths [Translated by Maria Adriana Veríssimo Varonese. Utilizando as competências das crianças. Porto Alegre: Artmed, 2001.]

COMTE-SPONVILLE, André. Translated by Eduardo Brandão. A felicidade, desesperadamente. São Paulo: Martins Fontes, 2001. [Happiness, Despairingly]

GARDNER, Howard. Five Minds for the Future [Translated by Roberto Cataldo Costa. Cinco mentes para o futuro. Porto Alegre: Artmed, 2007.]

HARRIS, Judy (org.); BENEKE, Sallee (org.). The Power of Projects: Meeting Contemporary Challenges in Early Childhood Classrooms – Strategies and Solutions [Translated by Vinicius Figueira. O poder dos projetos: novas estratégias e soluções para a educação infantil. Porto Alegre: Artmed, 2005.]

KRECHEVSKY, Mara. Project Spectrum: Preschool Assessment Handbook [Translated by Maria Adriana Veríssimo Varonese. Avaliação em educação infantil. Porto Alegre: Artmed, 2001.]

LAMA, Dalai. CUTLER, Howard C. The Art of Happiness: A Handbook for Living [Translated by Waldéa Barcellos. A arte da felicidade: um manual para a vida. São Paulo: Martins Fontes: 2000.]

MIZUKAMI, Maria da Graça Nicoletti. Ensino: as abordagens do processo. São Paulo: EPU, 1986;

MONTAIGNE, Michel de. Translated by Luís Leitão. Pequeno vademécum. Lisboa: Antígona, 2004.

PIAGET, Jean. The Origins of Intelligence in Children [Translated by Álvaro Cabral. O Nascimento da Inteligêcia na Criança. 4th ed. Rio de Janeiro: Zahar, 1970]

RIZZO, Gilda. Alfabetização Natural. 2nd ed. Rio de Janeiro: Bertrand Brasil, 2002.

ROUSSEAU, Jean-Jacques. Émile, or On Education [Translated by Roberto Leal Ferreira. Emílio, ou, da Educação. São Paulo: Martins Fontes, 2004.]

SEBARROJA, Jaume Carbonell et. al. (org.) Translated by Fátima Murad Pedagogias do século XX. Porto Alegre: Artmed, 2003.

SEMLER, Ricardo; DIMENSTEIN, Gilberto; COSTA, Antonio Gomes da. Escola sem sala de aula. Campinas: Papirus, 2004.

SEMLER, Ricardo. Você está louco: Uma vida administrada de outra forma. Rio de Janeiro: Rocco, 2006

SISTO, Fermino Fernandes, et. al. Dificuldades de Aprendizagem no Contexto Psicopedagógico. 5th ed. Petrópolis: Vozes, 2007.

TEBEROSKY, Ana; COLOMER, Teresa. Translated by Ana Maria Neto Machado. Aprender a ler e a escrever: Uma proposta construtivista. Porto Alegre: Artmed, 2003.

WEBER, Lídia. Eduque com carinho. 2nd ed. Curitiba: Juruá, 2007.

www.ingramcontent.com/pod-product-compliance
Lightning Source LLC
Chambersburg PA
CBHW060925040426
42445CB00011B/789